The
CONCLUSION
of the
WHOLE MATTER

CLARENCE SEXTON

CROWN
PUBLICATIONS
Royal Reading

The CONCLUSION of the WHOLE MATTER

CLARENCE SEXTON

FIRST EDITION
COPYRIGHT
MAY 2003

CROWN
PUBLICATIONS
Royal Reading

SUNDAY SCHOOL SERIES

THE CONCLUSION OF THE WHOLE MATTER

Copyright © 2003
Crown Publications
Powell, Tennessee 37849
ISBN: 1-58981-169-0
Layout and design by Stephen Troell & Joshua Tangeman

Printed in the United States of America

Dedication

*T*his book is affectionately dedicated to my two sons, Michael Shannon and Matthew Stephen. Shan and Matt are now both fine young men who love and serve the Lord Jesus Christ. They have beautiful families and enjoy their lives. Their mother and I know that they have learned the lessons of this book. Meaning in life is found only in Christ. They have concluded to *"fear God and keep His commandments."*

Clarence Sexton

Acts 5:42

Introduction

Imagine being the son of King David. There is no doubt that growing up around David's mighty men and hearing of the exploits of the shepherd king made quite an impression on Solomon's mind.

When David was king of Israel, his kingdom was marked by war and bloodshed. The king was a man after God's own heart, and there was only one serious black mark on David's record. It had to do with his adulterous relationship with Bathsheba and all the horrible things that followed. Of course, he sought God's forgiveness.

When the Bible says, *"The words of the Preacher, the son of David, king in Jerusalem,"* we know David had only one son who was king in Israel. His name was Solomon. He was a child born to Bathsheba and King David. King Solomon gives us this sermon about life without God.

The title *Ecclesiastes* means "preacher." There are twelve chapters in the book of Ecclesiastes. All twelve chapters combine to make one sermon. The preacher gives the introduction to this sermon in Ecclesiastes 1:1-3, *"The words of the Preacher, the son of David, king in Jerusalem. Vanity of vanities, saith the Preacher, vanity of vanities; all is vanity. What profit hath a man of all his labour which he taketh under the sun?"*

We find the conclusion to this sermon in Ecclesiastes 12:13-14, *"Let us hear the conclusion of the whole matter: Fear God, and keep his commandments: for this is the whole duty of man. For God shall bring every work into judgment, with every secret thing, whether it be good, or whether it be evil."* When God's Word says, *"the conclusion of the whole matter,"* He means *"the whole matter."* He said that the whole duty of man is to *"fear God and keep His commandments."*

Contents

"The words of the Preacher, the son of David, king in Jerusalem. Vanity of vanities, saith the Preacher, vanity of vanities; all is vanity. What profit hath a man of all his labour which he taketh under the sun?"

Ecclesiastes 1:1-3

Chapter One

THE EMPTY KING

he Bible is the Word of God, and God's Word is divided into thirty-nine books in the Old Testament and twenty-seven books in the New Testament. In the heart of the Old Testament, there are five books that deal with the great heart issues of man. These books are Job, Psalms, Proverbs, Ecclesiastes, and the Song of Solomon. These books do not deal with the national issues or great world-shaking events of the nation of Israel; instead, they deal with the heart issues of man.

The title *Ecclesiastes* means "preacher." There are twelve chapters in the book of Ecclesiastes. All twelve chapters combine to make one sermon. The preacher gives the introduction to this sermon in Ecclesiastes 1:1-3, *"The words of the Preacher, the son of David, king in Jerusalem. Vanity of vanities, saith the Preacher,*

vanity of vanities; all is vanity. What profit hath a man of all his labour which he taketh under the sun?"

Notice the expression in the first verse, *"king in Jerusalem."* We find in this book the life of the empty king. If we found a man somewhere in the kingdom of Israel, a man with absolutely nothing of this world's goods, and that gentleman said, "I have nothing; my life is empty," we would not be surprised. But in the book of Ecclesiastes, we go to the other extreme, to the palace of the king, in the time of the most glorious reign of any king, and King Solomon says, "My life is empty."

> *If we think we can be better, happier people by adding something else to our list of things, God has placed this book in the Bible to testify against us.*

This book deals with the subject of vanity or emptiness and the fact that only God can fill our lives. The word *vanity* or some form of the word *vanity* is used over thirty times in this one book of the Bible. *Vanity* means "vapor." A vapor is something we cannot grasp, something we cannot hold. The expression *"under the sun"* is found over twenty-five times in this one book of the Bible. *"Under the sun"* means "on this earth." With these expressions we find two keys to understanding this sermon. Solomon concluded that everything under the sun is vanity, that life on this earth apart from God is empty.

Imagine being the son of King David. There is no doubt that growing up around David's mighty men and hearing of the exploits of the shepherd king made quite an impression on Solomon's mind.

When David was king of Israel, his kingdom was marked by war and bloodshed. The king was a man after God's own heart, and there was only one serious black mark on David's record. It had to do with his adulterous relationship with Bathsheba and all the horrible things that followed.

When the Bible says, *"The words of the Preacher, the son of David, king in Jerusalem,"* we know David had only one son who was king in Israel. His name was Solomon. He was the child born to Bathsheba. King Solomon gives us this sermon about life without God.

We find the conclusion to this sermon in Ecclesiastes 12:13-14, *"Let us hear the conclusion of the whole matter: Fear God, and keep his commandments: for this is the whole duty of man. For God shall bring every work into judgment, with every secret thing, whether it be good, or whether it be evil."* This is the conclusion of the whole matter. God said that the whole duty of man is to fear Him and keep His commandments.

The last of the Ten Commandments that God gave Moses says, *"Thou shalt not covet."* Our nation is certainly guilty of violating this last commandment. We live for the pursuit of things. Materialism is the order of the day. We are a deceived, empty generation that has grown up in a materialistic society thinking that happiness and fulfillment can be found if we only have more things. The pursuit of things has left an empty world filled with people who have empty lives.

HE HAD EVERYTHING

The book of Ecclesiastes takes us to the palace where we find an empty king. We are looking at a man who had everything. Notice what Solomon said of himself in Ecclesiastes 2:10, *"And whatsoever mine eyes desired I kept not from them."* Everything Solomon wanted he got for himself. Anything his eyes beheld he got for himself.

The wisdom of Solomon and the glory of Solomon's throne was so far reaching that the queen of Sheba said, "I can't believe it. Nothing on this earth can be so magnificent and no man on this earth can be so wise." She traveled across the Arabian desert, went to the palace of King Solomon, and said as she stood in awe, *"Howbeit I believed not the words, until I came, and mine eyes had seen it; and, behold, the half was not told me: thy wisdom and prosperity exceedeth the fame which I heard"* (I Kings 10:7).

Speaking of Solomon, the Bible says in I Kings 10:27, *"And the king made silver to be in Jerusalem as stones."* This man's reign was filled with such wealth that silver was as stones. The soil in the land of Israel is full of stones; rocks are everywhere. In Solomon's day, silver was as the stones.

The Bible says in I Kings 11:3, *"And he had seven hundred wives, princesses, and three hundred concubines: and his wives turned away his heart."* Solomon had seven hundred wives and three hundred concubines. When he saw a woman he would like to have, he sent for her. When he married a princess, part of the marriage agreement was receiving a portion of what her father owned. Solomon's kingdom was enlarged because of this.

Solomon was a privileged man. His father was the famous King David. His throne was the mighty nation God raised up, the nation of Israel. His time period was a time of prosperity. Anything and everything the man wanted he had. The riches of the oil sheiks in the world today could not compare with the wealth of King Solomon.

Solomon had absolutely everything, humanly speaking, but his life was empty. Notice the testimony of this man in Ecclesiastes 2:17, *"Therefore I hated life."* If we think we can be better, happier people by adding something else to our list of things, God has placed this book in the Bible to testify against us.

HIS LIFE WAS EMPTY

Listen to the language of the Bible, *"Vanity of vanities, saith the Preacher, vanity of vanities, all is vanity."* The word *"vanity"* means "empty; vapor; nothing to be grasped, nothing to hold on to."

Solomon said, *"All is vanity."* If we took an inventory of Solomon's life, we would find that he was a brilliant man. He sought wisdom from God. He sat at the feet of King David and was taught by his father. He was an unusually blessed person. Solomon did not simply look at the birds and the beasts of the field, he became a zoologist. He did not simply observe plants and flowers; he became a botanist. He did not simply think about buildings; he became a great architect. He studied irrigation and established fountains and irrigation systems in his land. He was renowned among nations for all that he had and all that he could do. However, Solomon considered all that he had–all his stables, all his horses, all his buildings, all his wealth, all his wives, everything–and he said they were all vanity. He could not find fulfillment and peace in any of these things. All was vanity.

How many of us have surrounded ourselves with vanity? Many have built their lives on vanity. Many have filled their houses with vanity. Many live for the moment. One of these days, this will pierce their souls like a bolt of lightning from God Almighty. We all must realize we have only one life and we must not waste it on things.

NOTHING ON EARTH COULD SATISFY

Over twenty-five times, the expression, *"under the sun"* is found in Ecclesiastes. This means "earthly."

The quality of life I enjoy is beyond anything I ever dreamed I would enjoy. I need to be a better Christian and to be more satisfied with what I have. We are spoiled people. It seems that the more we get, the more we want to have.

Many good, godly people who love the Lord as much as anyone I know have very few things of this earth. It is a mistake to equate material gain and possessions with the blessing of God. Not everyone who has the things of this world has been blessed of God. If you think this way, you will believe that the people who do not have material possessions have not been blessed of God and are not living right.

Do you know what this earth has to look forward to? Fire. The house I live in will someday be ashes. The vehicle I drive will someday be ashes. The clothes I wear will someday be ashes. In II Peter 3:7-10 the Bible says,

> But the heavens and the earth, which are now, by the same word kept in store, reserved unto fire against the day of judgment and perdition of ungodly men. But, beloved, be not ignorant of this one thing, that one day is with the Lord as a thousand years, and a thousand years as one day. The Lord is not slack concerning his promise as some men count slackness; but is long-suffering to us-ward, not willing that any should perish, but that all should come to repentance. But the day of the Lord will come as a thief in the night; in the which the heavens shall pass away with a great noise, and the elements shall melt with fervent heat, the earth also and the works that are therein shall be burned up.

We are on this earth for such a short period of time. We must learn that we should not place our roots so deeply in this world. Solomon said that things under the sun, without God, will only leave a man empty.

WE WERE CREATED FOR ETERNITY

The Bible says in I John 2:15-17,

> Love not the world, neither the things that are in the world. If any man love the world, the love of the Father is not in him. For all that is in the world, the lust of the flesh, and the lust of the eyes, and the pride

16

of life, is not of the Father, but is of the world. And the world passeth away, and the lust thereof: but he that doeth the will of God abideth for ever.

God has created us spirit, soul, and body. If we neglect our spirit, which is to be the dwelling place of God, we will be empty people. God has so designed us that He dwells in our spirit and brings fulfillment. Without Him, we are empty. Without giving Him proper place, we have no joy. God has designed us so that we live and serve Him in time. While we are in time, it is the things that are eternal that bring fulfillment, happiness, peace, and joy. Remember we are all appointed to die. Alfred Lord Tennyson wrote in his poem "Crossing the Bar,"

>Sunset and evening star,
>And one clear call for me!
>And may there be no moaning of the bar,
>When I put out to sea,
>
>But such a tide as moving seems asleep,
>Too full for sound and foam,
>When that which drew from out the boundless deep
>Turns again home.
>
>Twilight and evening bell,
>And after that the dark!
>And may there be no sadness of farewell,
>When I embark;
>
>For though from out our bourne of Time and Place
>The flood may bear me far,
>I hope to see my Pilot face to face
>When I have crossed the bar.

If you have lived long enough, you can visit places and see things you once admired that are no longer quite as admirable. As you drive by the junkyard and see the scrap cars, remember that every one of those cars was once someone's pride and joy. The houses that are decaying were at one time the most beautiful houses anyone could find. These kinds of things should be sermons from God, telling us that eternity is coming. Heaven and earth are passing away. May we fix our hearts on Jesus Christ and on things that will count for eternity.

> *It is a mistake to equate material gain and possessions with the blessing of God.*

On the very practical side, we should make sure in our hearts that we know Jesus Christ as our Savior. We should make sure that there has been a time in our lives when we have asked God to forgive our sin and by faith received Christ as Savior. It is so important, more important than anything else, that we settle this one thing.

In the book of Philippians, the apostle Paul made a statement concerning Christ that drives the point home. Paul had everything. He was a religious leader. He was trained by the greatest teacher of his day. He could speak several languages fluently. He was a member of the most elite religious group on the face of the earth, and he was the most respected among that group. He was a Hebrew of the Hebrews, yet he wrote this testimony in Philippians 3:7-8,

> *But what things were gain to me, those I counted loss for Christ. Yea doubtless, and I count all things but loss for the excellency of the knowledge of Christ Jesus my Lord: for whom I have suffered the loss of all things, and do count them but dung, that I may win Christ.*

Paul said, "When I think of what I had, what I was called, and the prestige I enjoyed, following the Lord Jesus has cost me everything.

When I put it all on one side and Christ on the other side, all of it compared to Christ is but dung."

How precious is Christ to us? He cannot be as precious to us as He wants to be when other things mean as much to us as they do. He cannot be as dear to us when so many other things are as dear to us as they are.

Know Him as your Savior, serve Him through your local church, and determine to be used of God to get others involved in the Lord's work. Give your life to what is eternal by helping people know God and live for God. What does the Lord's work mean to you? It should mean more to you than it does at this present time.

Solomon, who had everything he wanted, was empty. On the earth, under the sun, nothing satisfies. Without God, there is no satisfaction. We can never be happy and find contentment and fulfillment without putting God in His proper place.

Remember, we have been made for eternity. We are going to live for eternity in heaven or in hell. The Lord Jesus wants us to trust Him as our Savior. This is the only way to get to heaven when we die. We should serve Him, live for Him, and invest our lives for Him.

When I was eighteen years old, God got hold of my heart. He had not let me know at that time that He wanted me to be a preacher, but I said, "Lord, I'm going to serve You." This may sound a little ridiculous because it is so simple, but I said, "I'm going to read my Bible every day. I'm going to go to every church service, Sunday morning, Sunday night, and Wednesday night for the rest of my life." Am I worse for that? Of course not!

I got serious about attending church. I decided to tell people about the Lord and give out gospel literature. I began handing out gospel tracts to people and trying to get them saved. I found a place in the church where I could serve God. I decided I was going to tithe. I was eighteen and had a young wife. I was attending college and paying my own way. Only God knows how we made it; but for all these years, I only regret that I have not given Him more.

If you do not know Christ as your Savior, trust the Lord Jesus Christ as your Savior today. Give Him the proper place in your life. Invest in the Lord's work. May the Lord help us not to live like the empty king.

"And I gave my heart to know wisdom, and to know madness and folly: I perceived that this also is vexation of spirit. For in much wisdom is much grief: and he that increaseth knowledge increaseth sorrow. I said in mine heart, Go to now, I will prove thee with mirth, therefore enjoy pleasure: and, behold, this also is vanity."

Ecclesiastes 1:17-2:1

Chapter Two

CREATED FOR PLEASURE

he entire book of Ecclesiastes is about life and the pursuits of man. One of the keys to understanding the message of this book is to understand the phrase *"under the sun."* Again and again, the preacher, King Solomon, reminds us that under the sun there is nothing new. Under the sun, upon this earth, there is nothing that satisfies. After plunging into life, trying to find something to satisfy, Solomon declares over thirty times that all is vanity. He finds only emptiness–this is life without Christ.

In Ecclesiastes 1:12-2:1 the Bible says,

> *I the Preacher was king over Israel in Jerusalem. And I gave my heart to seek and search out by wisdom concerning all things that are done under heaven: this sore travail hath God given to the sons of man to be exercised therewith. I have seen all the*

works that are done under the sun; and, behold, all is vanity and vexation of spirit. That which is crooked cannot be made straight: and that which is wanting cannot be numbered. I communed with mine own heart, saying, Lo, I am come to great estate, and have gotten more wisdom than all they that have been before me in Jerusalem: yea, my heart had great experience of wisdom and knowledge. And I gave my heart to know wisdom, and to know madness and folly: I perceived that this also is vexation of spirit. For in much wisdom is much grief: and he that increaseth knowledge increaseth sorrow. I said in mine heart, Go to now, I will prove thee with mirth, therefore enjoy pleasure: and, behold, this also is vanity.

In Ecclesiastes 1:17 Solomon said, *"I gave my heart to know wisdom, and to know madness and folly."* To whom or what have we given our hearts? In Ecclesiastes 2:1 Solomon said, *"Therefore enjoy pleasure."* Were we created for pleasure? The answer is yes, but for whose pleasure? The goal of the world is pleasure.

King Solomon writes here, *"I the Preacher was king over Israel in Jerusalem."* Solomon was the son of King David. He was probably the most privileged man who ever lived. The queen of Sheba heard about all that Solomon had in his kingdom, and she did not believe that anyone on earth could possess what was rumored of Solomon. She decided to go and see for herself. She made the long, strenuous journey across the desert. After hearing about all the magnificence of his kingdom, she arrived in the presence of Solomon and declared that the half had not been told.

Solomon lived for pleasure. He said in Ecclesiastes 1:13-15,

And I gave my heart to seek and search out by wisdom concerning all things that are done under

heaven: this sore travail hath God given to the sons of man to be exercised therewith. I have seen all the works that are done under the sun: and, behold, all is vanity and vexation of spirit. That which is crooked cannot be made straight: and that which is wanting cannot be numbered.

Solomon did not take a casual glance at things. He investigated, searched, and inquired. He did so much of this that he pushed his degree of intelligence as far as he could push it. He searched things out completely with everything that he could find available to help him understand the matter under investigation.

Here is a man who said that he had done more than anyone had ever done. He knew more than anyone, humanly speaking, has ever known, and he had more possessions than any man has ever had. After all of his searching and investigating, he came to this conclusion: *"that which is crooked cannot be made straight, and that which is wanting cannot be numbered."*

We are bound in life like prisoners in human shackles, and we can never be satisfied. In Ecclesiastes 2:1 Solomon said, *"Therefore enjoy pleasure."* By this he declared, "Do everything you can to satisfy the base feelings of your life and body because this is all the existence we have, this is all that life amounts to." In this world, we are surrounded by this philosophy.

We were created for pleasure, but notice whose pleasure. The Bible says in Revelation 4:11, *"Thou art worthy, O Lord, to receive glory and honour and power: for thou hast created all things, and for thy pleasure they are and were created."*

We were created for pleasure, but not to pursue our own pleasure. We were created for God's pleasure. In this journey we call life, we find that if we are constantly trying to satisfy ourselves, we will never be satisfied. We will always be looking for something else to give us gratification. However, if we come to the place where we seek God and seek to please God, He will bring joy and pleasure to our lives. Are we going to have to live and die and stand before God before we come to realize that we were created for His pleasure?

> *I was created for pleasure; not to seek my own pleasure, but to seek Him because I was created by Him for His pleasure.*

Everything functions best when it functions the way God designed it. He designed our lives to function a certain way with certain principles of moral decency. For example, He designed the family when He instituted the home in the Garden of Eden. He began the institution of marriage with Adam and Eve. He designed it a certain way–one woman, one man, one lifetime. He wrote things in His Book about whoredom, adultery, and other sins that violate the sacred institutions of marriage and the home. God has set the rules in order. If we seek to follow Him and realize that we were created for His pleasure, then pleasing Him will bring to us our greatest pleasure.

THE TRUTH CHANGED

I am using the language of the Bible when I say that the truth has been changed. Romans chapter one deals with the horrible degeneration of humanity. It moves from idolatry to immorality, where the perversion of life becomes the accepted lifestyle. In Romans 1:25 the Bible says, *"Who changed the truth of God into a lie, and worshipped and served the creature more than the Creator, who is blessed for ever. Amen."*

For the creature to be worshipped and served more than the Creator, the truth of God had to be changed. When God created

Adam and Eve in the Garden of Eden, the Creator was worshipped, not the creature. The Creator was served, not the creature. The truth changed. It does not mean that the truth actually changed. The truth still stands, but man is trying to change the truth of God. Truth is still truth, but man has turned it around.

In the Garden of Eden, Adam and Eve worshipped God. They knew that God and God alone should be worshipped. They understood that He is the Creator and that without Him they were nothing. In Genesis chapter three, when the Devil came to Adam and Eve in the Garden of Eden, he said, "Wait a minute! God isn't being entirely honest with you. He knows that if you eat of this forbidden fruit, you are going to be as gods. You're going to know good and evil, and you won't need God." Adam and Eve fell for that lie and sinned against God. They went into sin, and sin entered the bloodstream of all humanity. From that day to this, man in his natural state, which is sinful, seeks to please himself above all other things and motives.

If you ask the natural man why he is here, he will say, "I am only going through life once. I'm going to grab for everything I can, and I intend to do anything that thrills me. I am going to do whatever brings me pleasure." This is the kind of world in which we find ourselves living. The truth of God has been perverted.

THE TRAGIC CONSEQUENCE

The tragic consequence is that there is absolutely no possible way for a man who is living a lie to find satisfaction. All people need to hear the truth, see the truth lived, and know the truth.

There was a day in my life when I thought I was right side up, and the Lord Jesus let me know that I was really upside down. When He turned me right side up, it really turned me upside down from the way I was. He forgave my sin, came to live in me, and He has helped me to see that if I want to find satisfaction, purpose, and fulfillment and know true happiness in this life, I am to live for Him and not for me. I am to seek Him. My motive should be to please Him and not to please myself. I was created for pleasure; not to seek my own pleasure, but to seek Him because I was created by Him for His pleasure.

God's Word says in Hebrews 11:6, *"But without faith it is impossible to please him: for he that cometh to God must believe that he is, and that he is a rewarder of them that diligently seek him."* Without faith it is impossible to please God; so as we faith Him, or trust Him, we please Him. The Lord has so designed us that as we please Him, we will find our greatest joy and contentment.

Nearly three thousand teenagers every day in America contact a sexually-transmitted disease.

Solomon decided he was going to investigate everything he could about life. After all his investigating, he was convinced that if anything was crooked, it would never be made straight, and if anything was lacking or wanting, he could not find what it would take to satisfy it. Therefore, his advice was simply to enjoy pleasure. This is the lie of the Devil.

People in our nation and around the world are self-destructing by living for pleasure. Nearly three thousand teenagers every day in America contact a sexually-transmitted disease. Why? Because all that matters is what brings pleasure.

Paul wrote in I Timothy 5:6, *"But she that liveth in pleasure is dead while she liveth."* In other words, even though someone may be living in pleasure, God says he is dead while he is living. The tragic consequence of this philosophy is that when we change the truth into a lie and worship the creature more than the Creator, we have a living death.

We are told that when drug users get their first high, a certain quantity of drugs can be measured to bring that degree of thrill.

However, from that moment on, it takes a little more of the drug each time to reach the same level of high. The amount must be continually increased. God says that this constant craving to be satisfied, to be pleased, to bring pleasure, is self-destructing.

The Bible says in Titus 3:2-3, *"To speak evil of no man, to be no brawlers, but gentle, shewing all meekness unto all men. For we ourselves also were sometimes foolish, disobedient, deceived, serving divers lusts and pleasures, living in malice and envy, hateful, and hating one another."*

God says that there was a time when we served pleasure, when we only lived for pleasure. We say that pleasure served us, but this is not what the Bible says. The Bible says we stooped to the place that we would do anything for pleasure.

Why do you think the pornographic industry flourishes? According to *The New York Times,* Americans spend more than fourteen billion dollars on pornography annually. This is more than they spend on baseball, football, and basketball combined. This industry flourishes because of the philosophy that we live for pleasure.

The playboy philosophy could not exist without the philosophy that we live for pleasure. The tragic consequence is that it takes more and more until finally we are looking at a dead man who eventually winds up in hell forever because he lived to serve and worship the creature instead of the Creator.

TRUSTING CHRIST

The Bible says in Romans 8:32, *"He that spared not his own Son, but delivered him up for us all, how shall he not with him also freely give us all things?"* God says that if He were willing to give us His only begotten Son, He will also freely give us all things that we need. Do we believe this?

There was a day in my life when I asked the Lord to forgive my sin and by faith I received Him into my life. Before someone shared the gospel with me, I was confused about spiritual matters. I had the idea that some day God would put all the good things I had done on one side and all the bad things I had done on the other side. I honestly believed that if I had done more good than bad that God would let me into heaven. I do not know where this idea came from. I kept an eye on things, and if I got behind, I was going to make sure that I did some good works toward the end, if I could figure out when the end was coming. I was going to make sure that I had done more good than bad when the end came.

> *There is nothing worse than a Christless eternity.*

God's Word says, however, that *"all our righteousnesses are as filthy rags"* (Isaiah 64:6). The Bible says that *"all have sinned and come short of the glory of God"* (Romans 3:23). I am a sinner and my sin is against an infinite God. It deserves an infinite payment, which means to die and go to hell forever. There is no final payment as far as I am concerned because I am a finite creature trying to pay an infinite debt against an infinite God. I cannot do it.

Jesus Christ, who is God, came from heaven and became a man without ceasing to be God. He became a man, yet without sin. He never sinned. He owed no sin debt, but He could pay my sin debt. He went to Calvary and bled and died for my sins on the cross, and the holiness of God was satisfied by the death of Jesus Christ for my sin. He was buried and rose from the dead. He is alive forevermore. God accepted His payment. This is why He can be *"faithful and just to forgive us our sins, and to cleanse us from all unrighteousness"* (I John 1:9). This is what God did for me. If you do not know Christ, trust Him as your Savior, and the Bible says He will freely give you all things.

Created for Pleasure

The Lord Jesus said in Luke 12:30-31, *"For all these things do the nations of the world seek after: and your Father knoweth that ye have need of these things. But rather seek ye the kingdom of God; and all these things shall be added unto you."* May God in heaven help us not to seek the things of this earth, but to seek Him. May we not seek to please ourselves, but to please Him.

I am a happily married man. I have been married since February 15, 1967. I have two sons, two daughters-in-law, and six grandchildren. I thank God for the wonderful life I enjoy. However, I would hate to think about where I would be today if it had not been for Christ. I have had wonderful joy in my relationship with my wife and my children; but I have had it because of the Lord Jesus, not because of me. I have all this and heaven too.

In Luke 12:32 notice the tenderness of the Lord, *"Fear not, little flock; for it is your Father's good pleasure to give you the kingdom."* Just think of what God has in store for those who love Him. There is nothing worse in this world than living without Christ, then dying and going to hell. Do you believe that? Think about a home without Christ, a family without Christ, a husband without Christ, a mother without Christ, children without Christ. There is nothing worse than a Christless eternity. If this be true, it is also true that there is nothing better than living for Christ and going to heaven to be with Him forever.

We were created for pleasure; not to be constantly seeking our own pleasure, but seeking to please our heavenly Father. The Bible says that we were created for His pleasure. Anything in our lives that does not please the Lord Jesus should be given to Him and yielded to Him. He redeemed me by His precious blood. All of my life should be given to Him. In our homes, it is not enough to say that we are Christians. Christ must have the preeminence. We need Him. This world needs Him. Let us do all we can to please Him.

"For in much wisdom is much grief: and he that increaseth knowledge increaseth sorrow."

Ecclesiastes 1:18

THE SORROW OF KNOWLEDGE

 olomon said that he had investigated life. He found that he could not make the crooked straight. If he found something that was wanting, he could not bring it up where it should be. The more he learned, the more grieved he became; with increased knowledge, he found increased sorrow.

Years ago, I heard Dr. Vance Havner tell the story about traveling on a bus through the mountains of North Carolina with his lovely wife. They stopped at an old country store to get a soft drink. As they stepped back on the bus, Mrs. Havner said to her husband, "I don't think the folks in that store really know what is going on in the rest of the world." Dr. Havner's reply to her was, "Well, for goodness' sake, don't tell them."

If I said to you that I am going to deal with the subject of the knowledge of sorrow, you would understand what I intend to do.

You would understand that I am going to talk about sorrow, heartache, and the problems people have in this life. That would be the knowledge of sorrow. However, this is not the subject of Ecclesiastes 1:18. This verse does not deal with the *knowledge of sorrow,* but rather the *sorrow of knowledge.* God's Word says in Ecclesiastes 1:18, *"For in much wisdom is much grief: and he that increaseth knowledge increaseth sorrow."*

> *There is a certain loneliness in leading.*

One of the great burdens we bear is what could be referred to as the burden of knowledge. Solomon said that the more he learned, the worse he felt. The more he knew, the more grieved he became. He reached this conclusion before he made the Lord preeminent in his life. Many of us have said, "I wish I'd never found that out. It is so much more difficult for me to deal with this now that I know." There is sorrow in knowledge.

I remember being in a home where a death had taken place while one member of the family was away on a special excursion. This particular member was to arrive later in the day, and the family said to me, "We have not told her about this death." They had in mind that there was no reason to tell her about the death until she arrived. This knowledge would only increase her sorrow.

Perhaps you remember the story of a certain lady who participated in the winter Olympics. She had been in training and had been separated from her family for at least three weeks. She had not had any contact with home. During that time, a precious loved one died. Her family decided not to tell her until after she participated in her event because of the sorrow that knowledge would bring.

Some people who serve in certain capacities are privileged to information that they were never privileged to know before they began serving in that position. This does not mean that they find out things that are bad or immoral. But it is necessary for them to know certain things. Over the years in the ministry, I have heard people say that they wish they had never been in the position to hear these things. As a matter of fact, there are people who will not serve in certain positions because they do not want to be privileged to the kind of information that comes to those who serve.

There is a certain loneliness in leading. You have knowledge about particular matters that other people do not have, and you bear the burden of that knowledge in your heart. This can cause sorrow.

This is a day when much information is available to us. We are told that every few years the "bank of knowledge" doubles. We can turn on a television and span the globe. The media can bring the most horrible scenes of war, murder, death, and cruelty right into our homes. Sometimes, just knowing all those things makes us feel sorrowful.

Knowing the Person of Jesus Christ is where all knowledge begins.

Solomon had seven hundred wives and three hundred concubines. Think about trying to please one thousand women. Think of all the difficulties he had leading a nation. God had ordained that the nation of Israel be surrounded by other countries so that the influence of God upon His chosen people could be felt by others. Dealing with those nations, no doubt, brought increased knowledge and increased sorrow. The problems with his own country and the decisions he had to make were difficult.

In II Timothy 3:7, we see the conclusion God gives to our world apart from Him. He says that as far as learning is concerned, men are *"ever learning, and never able to come to the knowledge of the truth."* This means that it is possible to be formally educated and accumulate knowledge yet never know the truth. Jesus Christ said in

John 14:6, *"I am the way, the truth, and the life: no man cometh unto the Father, but by me."*

Often, as I am bombarded with things to think about, things to do, and things that are going wrong, I try to carry the whole load. The pull of people and their heartaches become burdensome. I understand what this verse means when it says that with increased knowledge, there is increased sorrow. At times, we want to retreat.

So much of our sorrow is caused by chasing after some thing or some answer and not following after Christ.

We all are nostalgic. We want to go back to a simpler time and a simpler place. We have in mind that if we could find a little cabin somewhere on the side of a mountain with a babbling brook running nearby, we could find serenity. This idea is a fairy tale. What we are searching for is not in a place, it is in a Person–Jesus Christ.

WHOM WE KNOW IS MORE IMPORTANT THAN WHAT WE KNOW

When we consider the subject of the sorrow of knowledge, we need to recognize certain things. The first thing is that whom we know is more important than what we know. Some people, when trying to climb the corporate ladder, might say that it is not what you know, but whom you know that counts. By this they mean that there is some personal connection inside the business that may open a door for them. What I mean is that knowing the Person of Jesus Christ is where all knowledge begins. If you do not know Him, everything you know becomes too great a burden to bear alone. Whom we know is more important than what we know.

People like to brag about what they know. We need to be grateful to God for Whom we know. In Colossians 2:3 the Bible says about the Lord Jesus, *"In whom are hid all the treasures of wisdom and knowledge."* From my vantage point as a Christian, I am looking at life through the eyes of faith in Christ as my personal Savior. From this point of view, I see all the sorrow in the world and I wonder how people live without Christ as their Savior. He is the great burden bearer. Where can I go but to the Lord? In Him are hid all the treasures of wisdom and knowledge.

Everything we need to know, we can find in the Lord Jesus. Everything we need to know about life, we find in Christ. Most people are in the great pursuit of knowledge in this particular period in history, but we need to pursue a Person. In Psalm 42:1 the Bible says, *"As the hart panteth after the water brooks, so panteth my soul after thee, O God."*

So much of our sorrow is caused by chasing after some thing or some answer and not following after Christ. I find refuge in the Lord Jesus Christ who will sustain me and give me wisdom to make the right decisions. You can do the same.

> *As we allow Jesus Christ to have His proper place in our lives, He will enable us to deal with whatever comes our way.*

This overwhelming sorrow of knowledge is what God sometimes uses to bring us to the Person of Jesus Christ. When we get so perplexed and weighed down that we think we cannot bear it, in our human weakness we are ready to admit that we need the Lord. We find out that Whom we know is much more important than what we know. When we take God out of the picture, life is more than we can handle. If we take God out of our homes and try to deal with our families alone, we have more than we can handle. If we take God out of our business and our business decisions, we have more than we can deal with. However, as we allow Jesus Christ to have His proper place in our lives, He will enable us to deal with whatever comes our way. Whom we know must always be more important than what we know.

In Matthew 16:13-17 we read,

> *When Jesus came into the coasts of Caesarea Philippi, he asked his disciples, saying, Whom do men say that I the Son of man am? And they said, Some say that thou art John the Baptist: some, Elias; and others, Jeremias, or one of the prophets. He saith unto them, But whom say ye that I am? And Simon Peter answered and said, Thou art the Christ, the Son of the living God. And Jesus answered and said unto him, Blessed art thou, Simon Bar-jona: for flesh and blood hath not revealed it unto thee, but my Father which is in heaven.*

Peter discovered who Jesus Christ is through the supernatural work of the Spirit of God. If you are a Christian, it is because God has done a supernatural work in your life–you have been born again. God's Word tells us how we can know Him in Ephesians 2:8-9, *"For by grace are ye saved through faith; and that not of yourselves: it is the gift of God: not of works, lest any man should boast."*

WHY WE KNOW IS MORE IMPORTANT THAN WHAT WE KNOW

Being involved in a Christian college, occasionally I meet young people who appear to be professional students. They have made a goal of learning without applying their education.

In I Corinthians 8:1 the Word of God says, *"Now as touching things offered unto idols, we know that we all have knowledge.*

Knowledge puffeth up, but charity edifieth." Simply gaining knowledge gives a person feelings that he can make it, he is in charge, and he is self-sufficient.

We should be learning, understanding, and having our hearts and minds filled with things so that we can use those things for the glory of God. Solomon was king in Israel. Everyone looked at him. But he was finding out that he hated life because he was empty. Knowledge had not filled his life, though he was full of knowledge. He was still not satisfied.

The Bible says in II Peter 1:3-5,

> *According as his divine power hath given unto us all things that pertain unto life and godliness, through the knowledge of him that hath called us to glory and virtue: whereby are given unto us exceeding great and precious promises: that by these ye might be partakers of the divine nature, having escaped the corruption that is in the world through lust. And beside this, giving all diligence, add to your faith virtue; and to virtue knowledge.*

The Bible says that we first have faith. After we ask God to forgive our sin and by faith trust Jesus Christ as Savior, we are to add virtue to our faith. Virtue has to do with what we are–character, decency, integrity, and boldness for God. Then we add knowledge. Adding knowledge without virtue is very dangerous.

Our world is full of knowledgeable people who have no virtue. They have no moral compass, no character, no honesty, no integrity, but they have knowledge.

When I surrendered my life to God to be a preacher, someone asked me, "Are you going to be a God-called preacher or an educated preacher?" That person thought that a preacher had to be one or the other. If God has called you, the calling of God is without repentance. The education you have received should never take the place of God in your life. Nothing you will ever learn can substitute for the power of God on your life. Why am I studying? Why am I reading? Why am I investigating? I do these things so I can be a better servant of Jesus Christ. The motive behind learning is so much more important than what we learn. If we get this turned around, we become dangerous to ourselves and to others.

WHAT WE DO WITH WHAT WE KNOW IS MORE IMPORTANT THAN WHAT WE KNOW

If we acted on what we know, we would move forward in our Christian lives. Think of how much we know that we have never put into practice. All people who are truly Christians know how to tell others of the Savior, but most have never even tried. People know how to pray but do not pray. People know the importance of the local church, but they do not love the church. Many know the importance of reaching children and doing something for God in the lives of others, yet they do nothing about it. What we do with what we know is more important than what we know. We are going to meet God with what we know and what we have done with that knowledge. May God help us to see this.

In II Corinthians 10:3-5 the Bible says,

> *For though we walk in the flesh, we do not war after the flesh: (for the weapons of our warfare are not carnal, but mighty through God to the pulling down of strong holds;) casting down imaginations, and every high thing that exalteth itself against the knowledge of God, and bringing into captivity every thought to the obedience of Christ.*

God says that we are to bring every thought to the obedience of Christ. If we know God and His Word, we are to live in obedience to that knowledge. God will hold us accountable for what we know and what we do with what we know.

I believe in education. I believe in knowledge. With the Lord's leading, I founded Crown College of the Bible to train people for the Lord's work. Our students are earning college degrees. There is a course of study that they must follow that is academically strenuous. They must complete it at a certain grade level to earn a degree. I believe in this. However, if this education is not given to Jesus Christ, it is dangerous. There is always the temptation for us to try to take the glory and the credit.

> *If Jesus Christ is our greatest knowledge, then knowledge can be a tremendous joy.*

I remember a certain group of people telling me about a business venture in which they got involved. They said, "We know God led us into this." I was so happy to hear that statement. Then they said, "God brought together so many able people." They began to tell me all the things that these people could do and how they had made this business what it was with their human ability. Without even knowing they were saying it, they were telling me that God got the glory for leading them into their venture, but they got the glory for making it a success. The Bible says in Deuteronomy 8:18, *"The LORD thy God...it is he that giveth thee power to get wealth."*

As a husband, you may say, "God brought this woman into my life. We are married and we are happy, and I have really worked hard to make this marriage all that it should be." The truth is, God has given you wisdom to be the right kind of husband or wife. God deserves the glory for any accomplishment in your marriage.

Solomon said that with increased knowledge is increased sorrow. Life does not have to be that way. If Jesus Christ is our greatest knowledge, then knowledge can be a tremendous joy. If the reason we are investigating and studying is to be more like Christ, knowledge does not bring sorrow. If we yield ourselves to God and let Him use what we know for His glory, knowledge is turned into joy. The difference is in what we do with the Lord. May God help us to yield our lives to Him.

"Then I looked on all the works that my hands had wrought, and on the labour that I had laboured to do: and, behold, all was vanity and vexation of spirit, and there was no profit under the sun."

Ecclesiastes 2:11

Chapter Four

IS THIS ALL THERE IS?

hat we find in the book of Ecclesiastes is not God's argument, but God's record of man's argument about the vanity of life without the Lord. Life without the Lord is empty. As you read through the chapters of this book of the Bible, over thirty times the preacher plunges into life and comes out saying, "I'm empty."

Ecclesiastes is a sermon given to us by Solomon, the son of David, the most privileged man to ever live. He was the king in Israel and son of the famous King David. Perhaps no man ever lived who had such expectation placed upon him.

God's Word says in Ecclesiastes 2:11, *"Then I looked on all the works that my hands had wrought, and on the labour that I had laboured to do: and, behold, all was vanity and vexation of spirit, and there was no profit under the sun."*

Here we see a man who said that anything he desired, he got for himself. Do you know anyone who has the power to do that? Can you imagine taking a walk through the most expensive stores, down the aisles displaying the most costly things, and being able to buy anything your eyes beheld? Can you imagine seeing any person you wanted to be with and being able to have him or her? Solomon lived this way. He said in Ecclesiastes 2:10, *"And whatsoever mine eyes desired I kept not from them, I withheld not my heart from any joy."*

Many people boast about their wealth and talk about their achievements. Solomon was a man who had everything he ever wanted, yet he said that without God he was empty.

Consider this question, "Is this all there is?" If you get your pockets full, your house full, your bank account full, and you get absolutely everything else you have ever desired, you are still an empty person if you do not have the Lord Jesus. This is the message of the book of Ecclesiastes.

The Bible says in I Timothy 6:6-7, *"But godliness with contentment is great gain. For we brought nothing into this world, and it is certain we can carry nothing out."* We are going out of this world to meet God with nothing but our naked souls. We will either know Jesus Christ as our personal Savior and have heaven as our home, or we will meet God not knowing His Son as our Savior and be in hell forever. This is taught in the Word of God, and our opinions do not change the Bible.

There is a real heaven and a real hell. Jesus Christ said that He is the only way to heaven. Salvation is not in church membership, baptism, or good works. Jesus Christ is the only way. We must ask Him by faith to forgive our sins and receive Him into our lives as our personal Savior. He is the only way to heaven, and He is the only One who can bring fulfillment to life on this earth. God has given us this record in Ecclesiastes.

In the end of the book of Ecclesiastes, the preacher comes to certain conclusions. He reaches his final conclusion in Ecclesiastes 12:13-14. He says,

> *Let us hear the conclusion of the whole matter: Fear God, and keep his commandments: for this is the whole duty of man. For God shall bring every work into judgment, with every secret thing, whether it be good, or whether it be evil.*

If a man could live and die and speak to us after death, he would say, "I'll give you this conclusion. The only thing that matters in life is to fear God, know God, live for Him, and keep His commandments." This is the conclusion of life.

What conclusions have we reached about life? At times we find that it is somewhat painful to come to a conclusion. However, we must come to conclusions about what we are going to do as far as our relationship and fellowship with the Lord Jesus Christ is concerned.

We need to find our conclusion about life from the Word of God. If we are going to reach an intelligent and faithful conclusion, we must heed this message. We have only one life to live, and it is gone so quickly.

An Empty Head

As we consider the question "Is this all there is?" we first see a king who filled his head, but his head was empty. The Bible says in Ecclesiastes 1:12-16,

> *I the Preacher was king over Israel in Jerusalem. And I gave my heart to seek and search out by wisdom concerning all things that are done under heaven: this sore travail hath God given to the sons*

of man to be exercised therewith. I have seen all the works that are done under the sun; and, behold, all is vanity and vexation of spirit. That which is crooked cannot be made straight: and that which is wanting cannot be numbered. I communed with mine own heart, saying, Lo, I am come to great estate, and have gotten more wisdom than all they that have been before me in Jerusalem: yea, my heart had great experience of wisdom and knowledge.

Here is a man who became a student of the things around him. He searched diligently to know things. He did not simply look at animals, he became a zoologist. He not only looked at plants, he became a botanist. He not only admired buildings, he became a great architect.

> *Salvation is not in church membership, baptism, or good works. Jesus Christ is the only way.*

You could look at Solomon and say that he was the most intelligent human being on earth. You have never had a professor who knew more than Solomon knew. Not only was he brilliant and gifted, but he also applied his brilliance to the greatest degree of seeking knowledge. He filled his head; then he said in verses seventeen and eighteen, *"I gave my heart to know wisdom, and to know madness and folly: I perceived that this also is vexation of spirit. For in much wisdom is much grief: and he that increaseth knowledge increaseth sorrow."* Solomon reached the conclusion that simply learning things and learning about things was not enough. He realized that the more he knew, the more sorrowful he became.

II Timothy 3:7 tells us that in the last days this world will be characterized by people who are *"ever learning, and never able to come to the knowledge of the truth."* In America, the largest single component in our gross national product is devoted to education. If education is the answer to life's problems, then the most serene, happy places on earth would be our university campuses. Just the opposite is true.

I certainly believe in education, but we are living in a crazy, mixed-up world where people have been convinced that gaining knowledge, ideas, and facts will make them happy. I have met some happy people at universities. I have met some fine Christian people on university campuses, but it takes more than the attainment of knowledge, facts, and ideas to bring purpose and fulfillment to one's life. Only the Lord Jesus Christ can do this.

King Solomon gathered more knowledge than any other man who ever lived. However, he said that, though he had filled his head, his head was still empty. Surely this is not all there is.

AN EMPTY HEART

Solomon also filled his heart, but his heart was empty. In Ecclesiastes 2:1-2 Solomon said, *"I said in mine heart, Go to now, I will prove thee with mirth, therefore enjoy pleasure: and, behold, this also is vanity. I said of laughter, It is mad: and of mirth, What doeth it?"* Solomon said that he was going to enjoy pleasure. The idea that pervades most of our thinking today is that we were created for pleasure. We were created for pleasure, but we must remember that we were created for God's pleasure, not our own.

People want to do away with or avoid anything that suppresses pleasure. Modern psychological ideas stress that anything that suppresses pleasure should be removed so that we can enjoy life. Solomon testified that he had seven hundred wives and three hundred concubines. These women were available to him, anytime he wanted them. He had pleasure.

Solomon's daily menu might interest you. It is recorded in I Kings 4:21-23,

> *And Solomon reigned over all kingdoms from the river unto the land of the Philistines, and unto the border of Egypt: they brought presents, and served Solomon all the days of his life. And Solomon's provision for one day was thirty measures of fine flour, and threescore measures of meal, ten fat oxen, and twenty oxen out of the pastures, and an hundred sheep, beside harts, and roebucks, and fallowdeer, and fatted fowl.*

This was one day's supply of food. Solomon dined quite well. He had anything he wanted to eat. He lived in pleasure.

Solomon also said in Ecclesiastes 2:10, *"And whatsoever mine eyes desired I kept not from them, I withheld not my heart from any joy; for my heart rejoiced in all my labour: and this was my portion of all my labour."*

Solomon was privileged above all men. He was king of the most peaceful, glorious reign in Israel's history. He could have anything he wanted. He said that he did everything he could to make himself laugh. As we study the expression of laughter in the early part of chapter two, we find that it has immoral overtones. Many so-called comedians today seek to bring laughter by talking about immoral things.

Solomon tried it all. He filled his heart with anything and everything he desired, including one thousand women, but his heart was still empty. We can believe the testimony of the Bible, or we can land on the wreckage heap of humanity and then testify that surely this is not all there is.

EMPTY HANDS

Solomon also filled his hands, but his hands were still empty. Many of us like to talk about what we have done. Some of us, especially men, are prone to associate success and value with achievements. Listen to Solomon in Ecclesiastes 2:4-5, *"I made me great works; I builded me houses; I planted me vineyards: I made me gardens and orchards, and I planted trees in them of all kind of fruits."*

Solomon had irrigation systems and pools that reached far beyond the normal technology of his day. He was far ahead of his time. He spent seven years building the temple. He built the palace of the cedars of Lebanon over the course of thirteen years. He built another palace for one of his wives. He built a great house and constructed military cities. Still today, tour guides in Israel point out stones that were laid by Solomon. He was a great builder, and he had no rival.

> *If education is the answer to life's problems, then the most serene, happy places on earth would be our university campuses.*

He thought that if he could not gain happiness in learning or in pleasure, he would gain it in achievement. He thought that he would achieve more than anyone else had ever achieved. His name would be inscribed in his works, and people would say of his achievements, "Look what Solomon built. Look what Solomon accomplished." It did not work. He remained an empty king.

The Bible says in I Kings 10:22, *"For the king had at sea a navy of Tharshish with the navy of Hiram: once in three years came the navy of Tharshish, bringing gold, and silver, ivory, and apes, and peacocks."*

Solomon had a navy at his disposal. He sent them to gather everything he desired. In I Kings 6:38 we see this expression about the temple, *"So was he seven years in building it."* In I Kings 7:1-2 the Bible says, *"But Solomon was building his own house thirteen years, and he finished all his house. He built also the house of the forest of Lebanon."*

Beholding such a man, one might say that it was impossible to achieve so much in a lifetime. Who could possess such a mind and such ambition? It seems unbelievable. Solomon thought that in achieving all these things he would be happy.

Perhaps you think that if you get the position or the promotion you are looking for, people may applaud what you have done, and this approval combined with achievement will bring happiness. Perhaps you think that a measure of success in the eyes of the world will bring satisfaction to your heart. This will never happen if you leave Christ out.

Some people live in the finest houses, drive the finest automobiles, wear the finest clothes, and dine on the finest meals, yet they lay their heads on their pillows at night and say, "Dear God in heaven, if there is a God, surely this is not all there is."

Solomon concluded in Ecclesiastes 2:11, *"Then I looked on all the works that my hands had wrought, and on the labour that I had laboured to do: and, behold, all was vanity and vexation of spirit, and there was no profit under the sun."*

The Lord Jesus said in John 10:10, *"I am come that they might have life, and that they might have it more abundantly."* Do you believe what Christ said? We are going to live and we are going to die if the Lord Jesus does not come soon. Our lives are winding down.

Believe Solomon's conclusion in Ecclesiastes 12:13-14, *"Fear God, and keep his commandments: for this is the whole duty of man. For God shall bring every work into judgment, with every secret thing, whether it be good, or whether it be evil."*

What have you concluded? Are you tired of thinking and talking only about what you are going to do? Look at your head. If the Lord Jesus is not preeminent in your thinking, you are empty.

Many of us waste our lives trying to entertain ourselves. We try to decide what we can do, where we can go, and where we can spend our money. If we are not living to bring pleasure to Jesus Christ, we are empty. If all we are doing is trying to achieve for the glory of achievement, we are empty.

May such deep conviction from God Almighty come over us that we will give the Lord Jesus His proper place in our lives. If you are not a child of God, invite the Lord Jesus Christ to be your personal Savior. Yield all of your life to Him.

"Therefore I hated life; because the work that is wrought under the sun is grievous unto me: for all is vanity and vexation of spirit. Yea, I hated all my labour which I had taken under the sun: because I should leave it unto the man that shall be after me."

Ecclesiastes 2:17-18

Chapter Five

WHAT MAKES A MAN HATE LIFE?

 ing Solomon came to the point where he said that he despaired of life and of all his labor. The French infidel Voltaire said, "I hate life, yet I am afraid to die." Many people feel this way. If you hate life, you more than likely live with the fear of death.

Solomon declared in Ecclesiastes 2:17, *"Therefore I hated life; because the work that is wrought under the sun is grievous unto me: for all is vanity and vexation of spirit."* What makes a man hate life? We should love the opportunity to live. In this passage we see the man whom I consider to be the most privileged man who ever lived. Without question, he was the wealthiest man who ever lived, yet he hated life. Solomon said that all is vanity and vexation of spirit. Everything was empty and exceedingly difficult.

Years ago, I came to know a fine young man who was training for the ministry. On the outside, everything looked beautiful. One day we received the news that this young man had ended his life by taking his automobile into a garage and breathing the fumes from his car. He left a note telling how he despaired life.

Not long after that, I read a story about a young man who had planned to graduate from the University of Michigan. His family went to the graduation exercise to see their son graduate. They could not get there early enough to greet him before the graduation exercise, so as they watched the ceremony, they looked for him. He did not appear. Of course, they were greatly alarmed by this, so they checked with the administration after the commencement was concluded. When they did, they learned that their son was not graduating. He had blundered some things in his course work and was not able to graduate. They were unaware of this problem. He was so disturbed about disappointing his family and about the fact that he was not graduating that he had disappeared three days before graduation. They found him; but when they did, he had taken his life.

> *The French infidel Voltaire said, "I hate life, yet I am afraid to die."*

According to the National Institute of Mental Health,

> The eighth leading cause of death in the United States is suicide. Specifically, 10.6 out of every 100,000 persons die by suicide. The total number of suicides is approximately 31,000, or 1.3 percent of all deaths. Approximately 500,000 people receive emergency room treatment as a result of attempted suicide each year.

You may get to the place where you say, "I am going to leave life. I am checking out." Think about what is beyond life. You cannot escape God by taking your life. Ending your life is never the answer.

You may never get to that point, but I speak regularly to many people who hate life. I think there are reasons for this hatred of life.

Many people wear beautiful smiles and know all the right things to do in public. In their public world, everything seems to be exactly in place; but in their private world where only God can see, their whole existence is falling apart. If life is ever going to be lived to its fullest, it must be reduced to our own personal accountability to God. This is where it all must start. We want to please others, but if life is going to be lived to its fullest, it must begin by being reduced to each individual and God.

As we look at Solomon's life, we discover some reasons why he said he hated life. At the end of this sermon, he says that the conclusion of the whole matter is to *"fear God and keep His commandments."* The conclusion of the whole matter is not what we are finding here at the beginning of the book. At this stage in his life, Solomon said that he hated life. Life was vain, empty, and vexing to him. It was exceedingly difficult for him to deal with life.

UNREALISTIC EXPECTATIONS

Solomon had the means to try anything and everything that he thought would satisfy him. He did not withhold himself from anything he desired. He had the expectation that having more would bring happiness. He believed that the more he gained, the happier he would be. He thought something or someone would bring him happiness and satisfaction in life. This was Solomon's expectation. There are millions of people like Solomon. As a matter of fact, I believe that all of us go through this stage. Some people live and die in this stage. We are very sincere about our expectation, but it is unrealistic.

A man may marry a certain lady and think, "This is the love of my life, and she is going to bring me total and absolute fulfillment." Then he finds out that as beautiful and wonderful as she is, he cannot find complete satisfaction in an individual. It just does not happen. Some people have the idea that if they get the next job, the next promotion, the next pay raise, if they make their way to the top in their business, they will find absolute fulfillment and happiness. Once they achieve all these things, they realize that there must be more to life than this. People live under unrealistic expectations.

Solomon became so disgusted that he said in Ecclesiastes 2:17-18,

> *Therefore I hated life; because the work that is wrought under the sun is grievous unto me: for all is vanity and vexation of spirit. Yea, I hated all my labour which I had taken under the sun: because I should leave it unto the man that shall be after me.*

It made Solomon angry to think that after all he had accomplished, he was going to die and leave it to someone else. If we live with the expectation that accumulating riches, building a name, or having things will bring us fulfillment and happiness, we are living with unrealistic expectations. If we live only for things, someday we will get disgusted about the fact that we are going to live and die, and all "our things" must be left to someone else.

This earth is a cistern, not a fountain. There are many things that can be accumulated here, but the satisfaction of the human heart can never be fulfilled by anything on this earth.

In I John 2:15-17 the Bible says,

> *Love not the world, neither the things that are in the world. If any man love the world, the love of the Father is not in him. For all that is in the world, the lust of the flesh, and the lust of the eyes, and the pride of life, is not of the Father, but is of the world. And the world passeth away, and the lust thereof: but he that doeth the will of God abideth for ever.*

Everything in this world passes away. If all we are doing is embracing the things of this world with the expectation that those things can bring us satisfaction and fulfillment, we are going to learn some day that all we have done is to embrace shadows. These things will all be gone.

Solomon set out to become and to have whatever he desired. He had one thousand women, he had exceeding wealth, he had a magnificent throne and kingdom, and he sincerely believed that all those things would make him happy. This unrealistic expectation that the search for happiness could be found in things, reputation, or achievement left the man so empty and so vexed that he said, *"I hated life."* We live in a world of empty kings. Many people have achieved much but hate life.

God says that we do not have to hate life; we can love life. We can enjoy living. Many of us torment ourselves with unrealistic expectations. God does not expect from us what we sometimes put on ourselves. We should be the best we can be for God, but we must find out what God wants us to do instead of what we want to do or what others want us to do. We can become so people-driven, achievement-driven, purpose-driven, or goal-oriented that we drive ourselves crazy and still do not do what God wants us to do. We need to ask ourselves what God's expectations are for our lives.

UNRESTRAINED DESIRE

We need to deal with restraining our desire for things. The natural man says, "If I want it and I can get it, I should get it. In getting what I desire, I will be gratified, satisfied, and fulfilled." Solomon was a man who got everything he desired. He put no restraint on his desire.

The Bible says in Ecclesiastes 2:10, *"And whatsoever mine eyes desired I kept not from them."* This unrestrained desire brought a hatred for life. It did not bring joy or satisfaction. Many of you have seen people who have wealth and means to do and accomplish things. It seems that many of these people are always chasing another car, house, or trip. You might think that if they got the finest thing in the world, they would be happy, but as soon as something finer comes along, they want it. They may move into a beautiful house and think it is wonderful, but as soon as something else nicer is erected somewhere across town, it is not long before they want that.

> *If life is ever going to be lived to its fullest, it must be reduced to our own personal accountability to God.*

When we fail to leash our desires, instead of making us happy, they make us hate life. This does not make sense to the natural man, but God had a purpose in this. In the very beginning, God put a restraint in the Garden of Eden. Genesis 2:15-17 says,

> *And the LORD God took the man, and put him into the garden of Eden to dress it and to keep it. And the LORD God commanded the man, saying, Of every tree of the garden thou mayest freely eat: but of the tree of the knowledge of good and evil, thou shalt not eat of it: for in the day that thou eatest thereof thou shalt surely die.*

A law without a penalty is nothing more than advice. God said that there was something to be restrained. There were things to be denied. The whole philosophy of the world is to deny yourself nothing. The world says, "If you can get it, get it. If you cannot afford it, go in debt for it. Just get it, because getting it will make you happy." God gave us a book in the Bible, the book of Ecclesiastes, to prove to us that unrestrained desire makes man miserable, not joyful.

Solomon was going to live it up. He felt that anything he wanted to do, he would do. I have talked to people who have given this testimony, "I have done it all." Instead of being happy, fulfilled, and excited they said, "There is nothing left to do. I cannot get excited about anything." Why? Because when we put no restraint on our desire, we will hate life.

As Christian people, if we say that this world is not our home, then why do we wish to make it so comfortable? Why do we want to drive our roots down so deeply when we say that we are just pilgrims passing through?

If we are going to love life, we must make the most of each day. God has wrapped life into twenty-four-hour packages. In Psalm 90:10, God talks about *"threescore years and ten; and if by reason of strength they be fourscore."* However, in Psalm 90:12 He said, *"So teach us to number our days."* According to God's plan, life is not lived in years; it is lived in days.

> *We live in a world of empty kings.*

We need not try to deal with our entire life at once. We can make plans, but we should not lose the enjoyment of today by planning for something years down the road. This is not the way God wants us to live.

We are so driven by the idea that one day everything will be perfect. We have the time marked, and we believe that when we finally arrive on that spot, everything will be wonderful. We may look forward to getting our children through high school or college or getting them out on their own. Why do we not enjoy them when they are two years old or in the first grade? We should enjoy them, not endure them, in every stage.

We can find the answer to this in I Peter 3:10-11, *"For he that will love life, and see good days, let him refrain his tongue from evil, and*

his lips that they speak no guile: let him eschew evil, and do good;
let him seek peace, and ensue it."

"Refrain His Tongue From Evil"

The Lord gives us a list of things in I Peter 3:10-11 that will enable
us to *"love life, and see good days."* He says that if we want to have
"good days," we must refrain our tongues from evil, and our lips
should speak no guile. What is the difference between lying and
guile? I tell our young people that honesty
is not the *best* policy, it is the *only* policy.
Guile means to exaggerate or embellish
the truth. If we have no guile, it means that
we speak exactly what is true. Guile is a
"cover-up."

A law without a
penalty is
nothing more
than advice.

Everyone of us could be happier if we
spoke less. Our tongues get us into
trouble. We are too quick to condemn things and people. Think about
how much happier our homes could be if we controlled our tongues.

"Eschew Evil"

The Bible also says that if we want to love life we are to *"eschew*
evil." This means we are to remove our feet from the path of evil. We
are to shun evil. We must understand our old nature. Our old nature
is a savage beast looking for evil things to get into. Our old nature is
on the prowl; it wants to find something to look at. If you flip through
the television channels and you land on something you should not
look at, your old nature wants to turn back and look at it again. We
are to remove our feet from the evil path. We must shun evil.

"Do Good"

We are also to *"do good."* You may say that you have done nothing
wrong, but what have you done right? Folks may say that they do not

hurt the church, the Lord, or their family, but what are they doing to help? The Bible says that we are to do good.

"SEEK PEACE"

We are also to *"seek peace."* The Lord Jesus said, *"Blessed are the peacemakers"* (Matthew 5:9). He did not use the word *peacekeepers,* but He said, *"the peacemakers."* It is not peace that we must keep, it is peace that we must make. There is war going on, and we must make peace. If we have an argument in the home, we should not try to see who can win. We should seek peace.

Solomon hated life because of unrealistic expectations that he placed on himself and the things he tried to have. He also hated life because of unrestrained desire; he would deny himself nothing.

UNYIELDED SPIRIT

Who deserves to be the authority in your life? Only the Lord Jesus Christ has earned the right. He earned this right by going to Calvary. He bled and died to pay our sin debt. He was buried and rose from the dead. He is God eternal, co-equal, co-existent, eternally existent with God the Father and God the Holy Spirit. The Lord Jesus came to earth and became a man without ceasing to be God. He has the right to be the authority. He is Lord of Lords.

You may say that you are in charge, but with that attitude you will never be happy. You will never have the fulfillment that only God can give. Solomon had to learn this lesson because he had an unyielded spirit. He hated life.

The Lord Jesus said in Luke 9:23-26,

> *And he said to them all, If any man will come after me, let him deny himself, and take up his cross daily, and follow me. For whosoever will save his life shall*

lose it: but whosoever will lose his life for my sake, the same shall save it. For what is a man advantaged, if he gain the whole world, and lose himself, or be cast away? For whosoever shall be ashamed of me and of my words, of him shall the Son of man be ashamed, when he shall come in his own glory, and in his Father's, and of the holy angels.

> *God gave us a book in the Bible, the book of Ecclesiastes, to prove to us that unrestrained desire makes man miserable, not joyful.*

The first thing on our list is to exalt self, but the first thing on the Lord's list is to deny self. He tells us that if we wish to keep our life, we must lose it. I want to be a happy man, but I have lived many days that I did not enjoy. I have had periods in life when I was miserable. Unrealistic expectations have made me miserable. I must get to the place where it is just God and me, and I must find out what God wants me to do.

We can drive ourselves and wear ourselves out, but it is not right to have the idea that doing things, whether good or bad, will bring joy. Only the Person of Jesus Christ brings joy and fulfillment. We also have unrestrained desires that can cause us to be unhappy. For those of us who have made up our minds about moral things, it is not always the immoral things of the world that draw us. We may not have the desire for someone else, but for something else, and we will not restrain that desire. There are many people who feel that they must have someone else. They keep going down the line trying to find that "one" who will satisfy. Sadly, it will never happen. God has made our lives so that we cannot be fulfilled if we try to use unrestrained desire. Not only will we be unfulfilled, but we will also hate life.

There is a constant struggle in our lives to decide who is going to be the boss. Jesus Christ must be in charge. We must ask Jesus Christ to come into our lives and forgive our sin; we must trust Him as our Savior. We must yield our lives to Christ and allow Him to direct our lives.

I am a happy man, but when I get these things out of order, I do not enjoy my life and when you let them get out of order in your life, you do not enjoy life. This is what the Word of God teaches. We may not live to be old, but we can make the most of every day God gives us. May the Lord help us to love Him and to love and encourage one another so that we never hate life.

"To every thing there is a season, and a time to every purpose under the heaven."

Ecclesiastes 3:1

Chapter Six

SEASONS OF LIFE

Life on earth has its seasons. The seasons come and go, but life goes on because God created us not only for time, but for eternity. God's Word says in Ecclesiastes 3:1-11,

To every thing there is a season, and a time to every purpose under the heaven: a time to be born, and a time to die; a time to plant, and a time to pluck up that which is planted; a time to kill, and a time to heal; a time to break down, and a time to build up; a time to weep, and a time to laugh; a time to mourn, and a time to dance; a time to cast away stones, and a time to gather stones together; a time to embrace, and a time to refrain from embracing; a time to get, and a time to lose; a time to keep, and a time to cast away; a

67

time to rend, and a time to sew; a time to keep silence, and a time to speak; a time to love, and a time to hate; a time of war, and a time of peace. What profit hath he that worketh in that wherein he laboureth? I have seen the travail, which God hath given to the sons of men to be exercised in it. He hath made every thing beautiful in his time: also he hath set the world in their heart, so that no man can find out the work that God maketh from the beginning to the end.

Did you know that God sends a message through everything that comes into our lives? The message is that we need God.

In these verses, we find fourteen contrasts. Time goes from one extreme to the other. There is no one emotion that sums up all of life. The longer we live, the more we have to deal with things that cannot be explained. It is beyond our ability to comprehend all that comes to us or to those we love. Those of us who are called into the ministry labor alongside people who are suffering greatly. It is especially difficult for us as we try to understand their suffering.

I remember receiving the news that a twenty-year-old son of a fine assistant pastor had taken his own life. This was hard for me to comprehend. One event after another in life challenges us to make sense of things that really make no sense.

Like King Solomon, there are things that we see and deal with that are most difficult. Solomon said that life is like the seasons. His argument is that everything apart from God is vanity. All of life is empty. As he plunged into life, he found that all is vanity.

THE INABILITY OF THE KING

We have seen this king as an empty man. Let us look at his inability. We see in Solomon a man who was powerful, humanly speaking. He sat on the throne of Israel. His kingdom was so wealthy that silver was as common as stones. He had seven hundred wives and three hundred concubines. The boundaries of his kingdom extended farther than they had ever extended. He was at peace with all those around him. He was so blessed with a marvelous mind that he is remembered even today for his wisdom. He was a builder beyond compare; he was an architect and a designer of great structures. He completed tremendous projects that in his day defied imagination and description. As he looked at his own life and the things happening to him, he was unable to change them. He was dealing with life and death, laughter and mourning. He was dealing with all kinds of things that he could not change. I am sure that as he reflected on his power as a king, he realized that he could not grant life or death in one command. He then thought about what he was unable to control in his own life. He thought about how he must respond to the circumstances that came to him. He thought about how little power he had over the course of his own life.

Did you know that God sends a message through everything that comes into our lives? The message is that we need God. We need God in birth and in death. We need God in planting and in plucking. In a time to kill or a time to heal, we need God. In a time to break down or a time to build, we need God. In a time to weep or a time to laugh, we need God. In a time to mourn or dance, we need God. We need God in a time to cast away stones, and in a time to gather stones. In a time to embrace, a time to refrain from embracing; a time to get, a time to lose; a time to keep, a time to cast away; a time to rend, a time to sew; a time to keep silence, a time to speak; a time to love, a time to hate; a time of war, a time of peace; in each and every situation in life, we need God.

In everything that comes to us, in every pain and ache in our body, in every circumstance that God allows to touch us, God sends a message, "You need Me. This journey is too great for you to make alone. It is too much for you to bear in your mind and human heart." In every season of life we need God! Dr. Al Smith put it this way:

> Tho' the seasons come and go,
> Summer's sun and winter's snow,
> Tho' the passing years to earth their changes lend,
> There is One whose love so free,
> For all time will changeless be,
> Jesus always is the same true friend!
>
> Then, while time speeds on it's way,
> Let us live from day to day,
> To be those on whom the Master can depend.
> For tho' nothing shall endure,
> Of this truth my heart is sure,
> Jesus always is the same true friend!
>
> Time's swift current onward glides,
> There is nothing which abides,
> Thru the fleeting years all things must surely end.
> Friends may fail or faithless be,
> But there's One who cares for me,
> Jesus always is the same true friend!
>
> Jesus is my dearest friend every day,
> Jesus is my dearest friend
> Come what may.
> Tongue or pen could never tell how much He loves me,
> Jesus is my true and dearest friend.

I remember standing at my father's grave as a fourteen year old. I knew so little about what was going on. All I knew was that my dad

was dead, and that our family needed help. I walked away from that graveside in Selma, Alabama, where we buried my father's body. Deep in my heart, though I could make no sense of what had taken place, I knew I needed God.

Sometimes we know we need Him and we do not know exactly how to find Him. It is these feelings of inability that help us to see that life is out of our control and that we need God. Even King Solomon came to this point and realized that he needed God. Every man and woman, every boy and girl, every human being on earth needs God. Dealing with the difficult circumstances in life brings us to realize our inability. Do you realize that you need the Lord? If you can keep trying, struggling, and scheming your way out of the trouble you are in, then God will use something else to help you realize how desperately you need Him.

THE INEVITABLENESS OF DEATH

Death cannot be avoided; it is inevitable. It is not hard for us to know the seasons. We may realize that we are in a season of sickness, a season of difficulty, or a season of decision. It is not hard for us to determine a season in life, but it is more difficult for us to determine the purpose of that season. We often ask, "Why has God allowed this?"

If Jesus Christ does not come soon, all of us will face death. The Bible says in Ecclesiastes 3:2, *"A time to be born, and a time to die."* There are some cultures that teach the philosophy of life that a man is not ready to live until he is ready to die. I really believe that in the Christian life, we are not ready to live as we should until we are ready to die. Until we know that we have made peace with God and have taken care of the inevitableness of death, we are not ready to live. The Bible says that *"it is appointed unto men once to die"* (Hebrews 9:27).

From the book of Genesis, we learn that we were created as immortal beings. We were created to live forever. Genesis 1:26-27 says,

> *And God said, Let us make man in our image, after our likeness: and let them have dominion over the fish of the sea, and over the fowl of the air, and over the cattle, and over all the earth, and over every creeping thing that creepeth upon the earth. So God created man in his own image, in the image of God created he him; male and female created he them.*

Every one of us will live as long as God lives. God made us this way. Before sin came into the Garden of Eden, man was going to live in the Garden of Eden in a dispensation of innocence forever.

The Bible says in Romans 5:12, *"Wherefore, as by one man sin entered into the world, and death by sin; and so death passed upon all men, for that all have sinned."* The Word of God says that because of sin, we are all under the sentence of death. It is foolish for us to talk about life as if we were going to live forever on this earth. When we start planting our roots so deeply in this world, as if this is all there is, we are living foolishly. The thing that makes this kind of talk foolish is the inevitableness of death. When we die, we are going to leave all our possessions behind. We must then stand before God with nothing but our naked souls.

Solomon sat on the throne of Israel and realized that he was just like everyone else. Although he was the king, he realized that he came into this world like everyone else and that he was going out like everyone else. If the Lord Jesus does not come quickly for those of us who are Christians, we too are going to die. Death is a gate to heaven or hell. When the gate opens, and it is going to open, you need to know where you are going. The only way to get to heaven is through Jesus Christ. I am so happy that He made the way clear. He

said in Ephesians 2:8-9, *"For by grace are ye saved through faith; and that not of yourselves: it is the gift of God: not of works, lest any man should boast."*

I am not going to heaven because I am the pastor of a church. I am not going to heaven because I am trying to serve the Lord with my life. I am going to heaven because when I was a teenager, after a Wednesday evening prayer meeting, someone took the Bible and explained that God loved me. He showed me that the Lord Jesus came to earth to bleed and die for me and that I was a lost sinner. He told me that if I would pray from my heart, ask God to forgive my sin, and by faith receive the Lord Jesus Christ as my Savior, He would come into my life, forgive my sin, and be my Savior forever. I bowed my unworthy head and was led in a prayer. I asked God

It is not hard for us to determine a season in life, but it is more difficult for us to determine the purpose of that season.

to forgive my sin and I trusted the Lord Jesus as my Savior. My name is now written in heaven. When the door of death swings open for me, I am going to heaven because the Lord Jesus made it possible.

THE INQUIRY INTO ETERNITY

In the third chapter of Ecclesiastes, fourteen contrasts are sandwiched between two great truths. The first verse of chapter three says, *"To every thing there is a season..."*

God has appointed a season for everything. People may say to me, "Why did my baby die?" or "Why did my baby get sick?" All I know is that they went through a season. The second part of the verse says, *"...and a time to every purpose under the heaven."* There is a divine purpose in every season of life. God knows the purpose. This is why we have to trust Him. It is beyond me, and it was beyond Solomon to comprehend all of life. My mind is not as far-reaching or as able as his mind was, and he realized that he could not grasp the meaning of everything in life. He came to the place where he simply had to trust God. We have all found ourselves there many times, and if we live, we will be there again. We may say, "Lord, I know I am going through this, but why?" This is where faith must enter in. We must say, "God, I give it to You. I know it is in Your purpose."

In contrast to verse one, Solomon said in verse eleven, *"He hath made every thing beautiful in his time."* Things do not always look beautiful to me. If you go into the kitchen where your mother is cooking, things may not look beautiful at the time you enter the room. However, when she puts the food on the table, it is beautiful. You may go into the sewing room and see something she is putting together. It may not look beautiful then, but when she is finished, the final product is beautiful.

Our timing is not always God's timing. When God finishes His work, it will be beautiful. We may not understand the pieces, but we must trust that the whole is going to be beautiful. This is the way God works. If we consider that God is late, it is because we are early.

Some precious people who have taken their baby's body to a graveside never knew at the time of their tears that they would have an opportunity to help so many others who were hurting. God has shown us that He is working all things together for our good and His glory.

He continues in verse eleven, *"Also he hath set the world in their heart, so that no man can find out the work that God maketh from the beginning to the end."* God has put in us an inquiry into eternity. Apart from God, we cannot understand anything that God is doing. We cannot understand life *"under the sun"* until we come to the Lord. God pulls the curtain and shows us that we have looked only at time. In that little season, our circumstances may not make much sense. However, He wants to show us that we were created for

eternity. We must believe that life after death is just as much life as life before death, except that the location changes. We who are saved will be with Jesus Christ forever. This life is so minute compared to eternity. We cannot imagine how long we will be with God. God has put the world in our hearts. He gave us an inquiring mind to want to know about eternal things. We realize that surely this life is not all there is.

> *God has put in us an inquiry into eternity.*

I remember sitting in the hospital with a dear Christian man who was dying. He looked at me and said, "Well, this is it." I said, "Yes, this is it." I wish you could have been with me as this godly man was leaving time and going into eternity. It would have helped you. It would have hurt your heart to see him look up to his wife and try to put a smile on his face, while his body was racked with such indescribable pain, and say, "I love you." He knew he was telling her that, on this side, for the last time. She answered, "I love you, too, Honey." I quoted every Bible verse that I could think of about heaven and the wonderful promises that God has given us. With every breath, he was asking God to help him with the pain. As I would begin quoting the verses, he would help me finish them. I said, "In just a little while the Lord Jesus is coming for you. You are going to close your eyes here and open them in His presence." His face lit up, and he said, "Oh, that will be wonderful!" The nurse came in, and he told her that he was in terrible pain. He wanted to rest, but he said that he did not want to go completely to sleep because he wanted to hear the birds singing when the Lord Jesus came to get him. He wanted to be awake until the last moment. He said, "I want my wife and my son here." The scene touched my heart deeply; it was so precious.

One moment this dear man was in the hospital room, and the next moment he was with Jesus Christ. I sat there, and I could have stayed, but I saw that there was just a little time left. I told his family that I was going to leave them alone for a moment. I told his son that if he wanted to say anything to his dad, he must say it quickly. I thank God that there was nothing that needed to be made right. There was just perfect love in this family.

Beyond the cross, there is an empty tomb. This world is not the end. The seasons come and go, but hallelujah, life goes on! For the Christian, it goes on for all eternity with the Lord Jesus.

"I know that, whatsoever God doeth, it shall be for ever: nothing can be put to it, nor anything taken from it: and God doeth it, that men should fear before him."

Ecclesiastes 3:14

Chapter Seven

IT SHALL BE FOREVER

he Word of God says in Ecclesiastes 3:14, *"I know that, whatsoever God doeth, it shall be for ever: nothing can be put to it, nor any thing taken from it: and God doeth it, that men should fear before him."* As we look at the expression, *"it shall be forever,"* we think about eternity.

We have learned as we walk through this book of Ecclesiastes that King Solomon, the son of David, is the human instrument God used to pen these words. The entire book of Ecclesiastes is a sermon. Solomon said that all of life is vain, that all is empty apart from God. He states that life without God has no purpose and no meaning. In this one sermon, over thirty times, Solomon says, *"Vanity of vanities, all is vanity."*

We are dealing with the matter of earth and eternity. If all we see is earthly and we do not see eternity, then what is happening in our lives will make no sense.

Why do we live the way we do? Let me speak for myself. I do what I do because I have eternity in view. My life is motivated by eternity. I have made decisions about what I am going to give myself to and devote my energy to because I have eternity in view. May this song be the prayer of our hearts:

> With eternity's values in view, Lord,
> With eternity's values in view;
> May I do each day's work for Jesus,
> With eternity's values in view.

If there is not an eternity, if life ends in death and we go into the ground and the worms eat our bodies and it is all over, then I am a fool. I am a fool because I have lived all of my adult life and plan to live the rest of my life with eternity in view. However, if eternity is real, if there is a real heaven and a real hell and Jesus Christ is the only way to miss hell and gain heaven, then my life has not been wasted. I believe that eternity is real.

In the book of Ecclesiastes God allows Solomon to give us a message, and in this message he talks about time. In Ecclesiastes 3:1 he said, *"To every thing there is a season, and a time to every purpose under the heaven."*

Many times we understand that we are going through a season, but we do not understand the purpose. We must know that there is not only an appointed season, but there is also a determined purpose. People may realize that they are going through a season of suffering, mourning, confusion, frustration, or searching; however, they do not understand the purpose. They may wonder why God is allowing them to go through this season.

Solomon goes on to tell that there is a time for each purpose, and he gives fourteen different contrasts about time. Then suddenly God interrupts in verse fourteen, and we move from time to the thought of eternity. This is the way our lives must be. Sometimes life seems to be nothing but a cycle. We have one thing happen after another, and we wonder what is going on. Nothing seems to make sense, and then suddenly God breaks in somewhere, and we must think about eternity. We realize that this is not the end of it all. Heaven is real. The Lord Jesus is real. There is more to life than the present.

A STATEMENT OF FACT

We may deny the fact of eternity, but our denial will not change the truth. In Ecclesiastes 3:14 the Bible says, *"I know that, whatsoever God doeth, it shall be for ever."* The writer says, *"I know."* Eternity is a fact.

Our lives started with conception. Nine months later, we were brought forth into the world from our mother's womb. All of us in this world came into the world through natural birth. Adam and Eve got here by direct creation, and Jesus Christ by the virgin birth. We came forth by what we call natural birth, which really is supernatural. We have a certain number of days appointed to us in this life, as far as time is concerned. But beyond this life, when we depart through the gate of death to heaven or hell, we will live forever, because eternity is real. When we come to the gate of death, we have already decided somewhere in life whether we are going to heaven or hell. This has been determined by what we have done with Jesus Christ. Receiving Him as Savior means heaven. It is a statement of fact that *"whatsoever God doeth, it shall be for ever."* We are dealing with an eternal God, an eternal Book, an eternal existence, and an eternal dwelling. Eternity is real.

In Genesis 1:1 the Bible says, *"In the beginning, God created the heaven and the earth."* God had no beginning, and he has no ending. He is eternal God–no beginning, no ending, no middle. Our Lord says in Revelation 1:17-18, *"I am the first and the last: I am he that liveth, and was dead; and behold, I am alive for evermore, Amen; and have the keys of hell and of death."*

> *Many times we understand that we are going through a season, but we do not understand the purpose. We must know that there is not only an appointed season, but there is also a determined purpose.*

The Lord is not talking about having a beginning. When the Bible says in John 1:11 that Jesus Christ *"came"* into this world, God is telling us by the very use of the word *came* that He existed before He came. When God speaks in reference to time, He is not speaking of Himself being confined by time; He is doing this for our benefit, to help us understand. God is eternal. This is beyond our comprehension. With our finite minds, we cannot grasp eternity. But the Bible says that *"whatsoever God doeth, it shall be for ever."*

The Bible says in Psalm 33:11, *"The counsel of the LORD standeth for ever, the thoughts of his heart to all generations."* We are dealing with the God of eternity. Solomon looked at the palace he had built, the temple he had constructed, and all the things he had done. People traveled great distances to see him because they did not believe what they had heard. However, when they arrived, they said that the half had never been told. Men marvelled at the works of his hands. Then Solomon realized that all that he had done was for time, but *"whatsoever God doeth, it shall be for ever."* When we look at the accomplishments of our hands, we must always be reminded that our works only last for a time, but *"whatsoever God doeth, it shall be for ever."*

In Isaiah 46:9-10 the Bible says,

> *Remember the former things of old: for I am God, and there is none else; I am God, and there is none like me, declaring the end from the beginning, and from ancient times the things that are not yet done, saying, My counsel shall stand, and I will do all my pleasure.*

God says, "I am eternal God. I know how human history started; I know how human history will end. I stretch beyond its beginning and ending. I can declare the things that are not yet done before they ever take place. I am God eternal, and there is none else." This is a statement of fact.

The Bible says in Isaiah 51:6,

> *Lift up your eyes to the heavens, and look upon the earth beneath: for the heavens shall vanish away like smoke, and the earth shall wax old like a garment, and they that dwell therein shall die in like manner: but my salvation shall be for ever, and my righteousness shall not be abolished.*

Walk out on some clear night and look at the starry galaxies above. Look at the heavens, then look at the earth beneath. Look at all the people upon the earth. God says, "It is all going to vanish away, but My salvation shall be forever. My righteousness shall not be abolished."

A STATEMENT OF FAITH

Notice again what Solomon said in Ecclesiastes 3:14, *"I know that, whatsoever God doeth, it shall be for ever: nothing can be put to it, nor any thing taken from it."*

Sometimes when we refer to salvation, we say that our salvation is by the grace of God through faith, plus nothing, minus nothing. Have you ever heard that? Solomon said that *"nothing can be put to it, nor any thing taken from it."* In other words, *"Whatsoever God doeth, it shall be for ever."* We cannot add anything to it or take anything from it. God has a purpose. This is a statement of faith.

Faith is coming to a place where we believe God and take Him at His Word. We do not attempt to help God out. We are all guilty of the sin of trying to help God be God. Peter was guilty of this. When the Lord Jesus announced to His disciples that He was going to go to the cross and die, Peter said, "No, wait a minute. It shall not be so." Christ said, *"Get thee behind me, Satan"* (Matthew 16:23). It is just as wicked for us to try to add to or take away from God's plan and purpose.

Jesus Christ came into the world to seek and save that which was lost. The Bible says in John 3:16, *"For God so loved the world, that he gave his only begotten Son, that whosoever believeth in him should not perish, but have everlasting life."*

Jesus Christ came to this earth and lived a sinless life. Because He never sinned, He owed no sin debt. We are sinners, and we owe a sin debt. The wages of our sin is death and hell, separation from God forever. Jesus Christ never sinned. When He came to the cross of Calvary, He bore the sins of the whole world upon Himself. God's Word says in Hebrews 2:9, *"But we see Jesus, who was made a little lower than the angels for the suffering of death, crowned with glory and honour; that he by the grace of God should taste death for every man."* You may say, "What about my future sins?" Friends, when Christ died, all our sins were future. He died for all sin, for all time, for all people. He paid the sin debt for us all. He bore the sins of the whole world upon Himself. He satisfied the just demand of a holy God that every human being is a sinner, and every human being's sin must be paid for. A just, holy God said that it must be done. Jesus

Christ paid the debt. In doing so, He satisfied the justice of God. He was buried, and He rose from the dead.

As He was dying, Jesus Christ said in John 19:30, *"It is finished."* Notice that He did not say, "I am finished"; He said, *"It is finished."* What is finished? God's plan of salvation is finished. You cannot add anything to it or take anything away from it. It is finished! This is what God demanded, that the debt of sin must be paid. Salvation is all of grace by faith. No wonder the Bible says in Ephesians 2:8-9, *"For by grace are ye saved through faith; and that not of yourselves: it is the gift of God: not of works, lest any man should boast."*

> *Solomon realized that all that he had done was for time, but "whatsoever God doeth, it shall be for ever."*

People may say that they want to help God out. God says that salvation is *"not of works, lest any man should boast."* There is nothing that we can offer Him. For us to try to add something to salvation is like walking up to God and saying that Christ did not do all that He needed to do. God forbid that we would ever have that attitude. We are to humble ourselves before God as hell-deserving, wretched sinners.

By the way, this old nature of ours does not like this thought. By our very nature, we want to help God out. It makes us feel better. It makes us look better. The songwriter was right when he wrote, "Nothing in my hand I bring, simply to Thy cross I cling." Salvation is of the Lord. Nothing can be added to it. Nothing can be taken from it.

As believers, we are to live a faith life. Do you understand how this works? People may say, "You don't understand. I'm living for now. I'm excited about now. I've got everything going for me now." If you watch how they live, how they talk, and what they invest their money in, this is exactly what they are doing. They only live for now.

They live as though they are going to live here forever. We are all guilty of this.

In Hebrews 11:3 the Bible says, *"Through faith, we understand that the worlds were framed by the word of God, so that things which are seen were not made of things which do appear."* This is a verse about creation. God said that He spoke the worlds into existence. It is even hard for Christian people to understand this, but we believe it by faith. Nothing existed, and God spoke the worlds into existence.

In Hebrews 11:13 the Bible says, *"These all died in faith, not having received the promises, but having seen them afar off, and were persuaded of them, and embraced them, and confessed that they were strangers and pilgrims on the earth."*

Why did God's people live like this? They lived like this because they had faith in the fact of eternity. If there is no such thing in the world as eternity, then the most foolish thing that you can do is to live for God. We are in time, but we are headed for eternity. Our eternal souls need help, instruction, and understanding. We need to live with eternity in view. We not only need to learn how to live our daily lives when things are normal, but we also need to know how to make sense of tragedy and heartache in life when things are not, as we say, "going normal." The only way we can do this is to have eternity in view.

The Bible says in I Peter 4:12-13, *"Beloved, think it not strange concerning the fiery trial which is to try you, as though some strange thing happened to you: but rejoice, inasmuch as ye are partakers of Christ's sufferings; that, when his glory shall be revealed, ye may be glad also with exceeding joy."*

The word *"strange"* here means "that which does not belong to us." We could read this as, "Don't think this does not belong to you." You may say, "I am trying to live for God. Why am I having trouble?" Someone might say, "Why do I have cancer? Why is my wife dying?

Why did my baby die? I am trying to go to church and do what is right. This is not supposed to belong to me." Wait a minute. You did not get that from the Bible. The only way you can handle heartache is with eternity in view. Do not think that the fiery trial does not belong to you, that suffering is not supposed to come to you. This is not what the Bible teaches.

> *We are all guilty of the sin of trying to help God be God.*

When trials are taking place here and now, the only way we can live is by faith. We certainly do not always understand. It hurts me to see daddies cry about their children. It breaks my heart. I think sometimes, "How can they be victorious?" I just keep telling them that God is working.

The last part of I Peter 4:13 says again, *"...when his glory shall be revealed..."* For those who have put their faith in God in the difficult times, when nothing seemed to make sense, there is going to be something special when He appears. This is what the Bible says, *"...that when his glory shall be revealed, ye may be glad also with exceeding joy."*

It is as though God says, "I have helped you through it now, but I have saved the best until last." You may feel that the season you went through was terrible. You could not understand the purpose, but when you see your blessed Savior and He makes known to you His eternal purpose, you will have exceeding joy. Then you will see how He tied all the pieces together.

A STATEMENT OF FEAR

We do not like the word *fear,* but it is a Bible word. Solomon said in Ecclesiastes 3:14, *"I know that, whatsoever God doeth, it shall be for ever: nothing can be put to it, nor any thing taken from it: and God doeth it, that men should fear before him."*

Notice that he says, *"That men should fear before him."* This is also a statement about fear. What does this mean? It means that as I face the fact of eternity, and as I put my faith in the Lord, I fear God. He is God, and there is none else. The Lord is still the Lord in my life. He is still in charge. He is still in control. He is still Almighty God. I am not going to let anything blow me off course. I still feel the same way about God.

What do you think the Devil tries to do when something goes wrong and we cannot understand it? He tries to get us to think differently about God. He may say, "God hasn't been good to you. He could have prevented this death. Your loved one didn't have to get cancer. Many people more wicked than your loved one are out running around, strong as can be. Why did God not take one of them? God could have been better to you than He has been." Satan tries to get us to think differently about God.

In Revelation 15:3-4 the Bible says,

> *And they sing the song of Moses the servant of God, and the song of the Lamb, saying, Great and marvellous are thy works, Lord God Almighty; just and true are thy ways, thou King of saints. Who shall not fear thee, O Lord, and glorify thy name? for thou only art holy: for all nations shall come and worship before thee; for thy judgments are made manifest.*

We will live by sight in heaven, but now we must have faith. There is coming a day when God will pull back the curtain, and we will see everything. His judgments will be made manifest. Speaking of this time, the Bible says, *"Who shall not fear thee, O Lord, and glorify thy name?"* We do not have to wait until all things are revealed before we treat God as He should be treated. By faith we must fear

God and give the Lord His proper place in our lives. This is what this message in Ecclesiastes 3:14 is all about.

The Bible says, *"It shall be for ever."* This is fact. Put your faith in Him. Do not try to add anything to your faith or take anything away from it. Put your faith in God, and do not let anything that happens to you change what you believe about God. Fear Him, honor Him, and obey Him.

I hope that you know Christ as your personal Savior. If you do not know Him, you need to trust Him as your Savior. Time is fading. Your life is being wasted. If you do know him as your Savior, stop being a nominal Christian. Some day, the veil will be removed and we will see beyond this veil of tears. We will see beyond earthly things, and we will be made aware of the wicked world that exists. When God reveals Himself in mighty power, we are going to wonder why we did not live for the Lord Jesus while we were here on earth. May the Lord help us to live for Him, honor Him, and obey Him now.

"So I returned, and considered all the oppressions that are done under the sun: and behold the tears of such as were oppressed, and they had no comforter; and on the side of their oppressors there was power; but they had no comforter. Wherefore I praised the dead which are already dead more than the living which are yet alive. Yea, better is he than both they, which hath not yet been, who hath not seen the evil work that is done under the sun."

Ecclesiastes 4:1-3

Chapter Eight

BEHOLD THE TEARS

he Word of God says in Ecclesiastes 4:1, *"Behold the tears."* As Solomon looked upon the people of his kingdom, the first thing he said was that he saw their tears. The Word of God says in Job 14:1, *"Man that is born of a woman is of few days, and full of trouble."* Most of us start out in life thinking that we are going to be one of the few who do not have much heartache with which to deal. I have met many unsuspecting people who are dealing with tragic things.

It is good for us, as we walk through life, to *"behold the tears."* It does something for us. It helps us to understand the real priorities in life. Beholding the tears helps us minimize the value of worldly possessions. It helps us avoid driving our roots too deeply into this world.

We cannot talk about life without talking about weeping and sadness. We cannot observe life without observing the tears. It is no wonder the Bible says, *"Behold the tears."*

Consider what King Solomon said in Ecclesiastes 4:1 as he looked out over the people, *"So I returned, and considered all the oppressions that are done under the sun: and behold the tears of such as were oppressed, and they had no comforter; and on the side of their oppressors there was power; but they had no comforter."*

THE CONSIDERATIONS

The king *"considered all the oppressions."* Under the sun, apart from God, Solomon could see so much oppression and so many problems. On the side of the oppression, there was much power, and the people had no comforter. They had no one to help them. Solomon said that even though he was king over Israel, he was unable to comfort them. They had no human help, no comforter, and so he gives these considerations. They are the same sad considerations that people are making today. He said in Ecclesiastes 4:2, *"Wherefore I praised the dead which are already dead more than the living which are yet alive."*

His first consideration was that it was bad to live. His second consideration was that it was better to die. Every time we pick up the newspaper, we read about death and suicide, especially the increasing number of suicides. This onslaught of suicide is directly connected to the secularization of our nation and the neglect of God in life. As we move farther from God and godliness and lose sight of any great purpose for living, we are going to see more and more of the tragedy of suicide.

King Solomon said that under the sun he thought it was bad to live because the oppressors had all the power. It would be better to die. He also said in Ecclesiastes 4:3, *"Yea, better is he than both they, which hath not yet been, who hath not seen the evil work that is done under the sun."*

He felt that without knowing the Lord, it was bad to live, it was better to die, but it was best to have never been born. Think of this:

> Bad to live
> Better to die
> Best to have never been born

This is where life without God leads. Not everyone may express it exactly this way, but in this fourth chapter of Ecclesiastes, this is the way God allows us to see it. Under the sun, everything is vanity and life is only bad. Death is better than living, and it is best to have never been born. Have you ever felt this way? Have you ever felt that life is bad, that it would be better to die, and that it would be best if you had never been born? If you do not feel this way, do you know anyone else who feels this way? If you know someone who feels this way about life or if you feel this way about life, there is a reason for it.

Beholding the tears helps us minimize the value of worldly possessions.

The person who thinks this way is considering life under the sun without Jesus Christ and the truth of His Word. Wrapped up in its own package, life is bad. Sometimes it seems that we would be greatly relieved to die, and we would be better off if we had never been born. These are the considerations that are given in this passage.

THE COMFORTER

Solomon said, *"They had no comforter."* Solomon said that life was bad because oppression was upon people, and the oppressors had power. Under the sun, apart from God, there is no comforter. We know that without Jesus Christ, there is no true comforter. It is a terrible thing to go through life without God's help. It is tragic for people who know the Lord to live as though they have no help. Have you trusted the Lord as your personal Savior? Do you know that there was a time in your life when you asked the Lord to forgive your sin and by faith you received Jesus Christ as your Savior? There is only one way to heaven. Jesus Christ said in John 14:6, *"I am the way, the truth, and the life: no man cometh unto the Father, but by me."*

We should rejoice more and more with each passing day that we have the Son of God as our Savior. We have a Comforter. The world without God is hopelessly sad and heartbroken. People have nothing but tears.

> *It is tragic for people who know the Lord to live as though they have no help.*

The Bible says in Revelation 21:4, *"And God shall wipe away all tears from their eyes; and there shall be no more death, neither sorrow, nor crying, neither shall there be any more pain: for the former things are passed away."* We have the great hope that some day the hand of God will wipe away all the tears of His children. This is for the saved; but for the lost, the Bible says that for eternity there shall be weeping and gnashing of teeth. Those who do not know the Lord Jesus shall be without God and without hope for eternity. It is a terrible thing to live without the Lord, and have no Comforter; but it is even more horrible to die without Him. We have a Comforter; His name is Jesus Christ.

In Isaiah 25:8 the Bible says, *"He will swallow up death in victory; and the Lord GOD will wipe away tears from off all faces; and the rebuke of his people shall he take away from off all the earth: for the LORD hath spoken it."*

We should thank God that we have a Comforter. Go with me to the hospital room just after the doctor has been in to tell the patient that he has cancer. What are we going to say? Walk with me through a hospital ward past room after room with newborn babies and their mothers and then walk into the room where there is no newborn. Death has come to a newborn. What are we going to tell the parents? We have a Comforter. We have a Savior. It is beyond me to try to understand how people are living on earth without the Lord Jesus. In reality, they are not. The power is on the side of the oppressor. No wonder they want to die. No wonder they wish they had never lived. We have a Comforter; let us rush to Him and lean on Him. I often use the expression, "Let's lean heavily on the Savior." I think that I am not merely leaning on Him, I am clinging to Him. We have a Comforter who wipes away the tears.

The Lord Jesus shares a beautiful lesson with us in John chapter sixteen. He was going to Calvary to bleed and die, and His disciples loved Him very much. He had walked with them and talked with them. They wanted Him. He said to them in John 16:5-7,

> *But now I go my way to him that sent me; and none of you asketh me, Whither goest thou? But because I have said these things unto you, sorrow hath filled your heart. Nevertheless I tell you the truth; It is expedient for you that I go away: for if I go not away, the Comforter will not come unto you; but if I depart, I will send him unto you.*

The word *"expedient"* means "in your best interest." He told them that it was in their best interest that He go away. They must have wondered how that could be. The Son of God was with them, in person, talking to them. They loved Him and needed Him. They felt that they could not live without Him. He then tells them that it is in their best interest for Him to leave them.

When Jesus Christ was on this earth, He was limited by bodily form, robed in flesh. He went to Calvary, bled and died for our sins, was buried in a borrowed tomb, and came forth from the grave. He ascended to heaven and sat down at the right hand of God the Father. Now, the Holy Spirit of God has come to indwell believers forever. He is not limited by location; He can be everywhere at the same time. This means that people in Asia can have Jesus Christ and people in America can have Jesus Christ. People in Africa can have Jesus Christ and people in Europe can have Jesus Christ. People across the street can have Jesus Christ and people in your house can have Jesus Christ. People in every church where the Bible is preached and God is honored can have Jesus Christ, and we can have Jesus Christ. It means that every one of us can have the Lord Jesus Christ personally as His work continues in the Person of the Holy Spirit.

> *It would be better to have one hand full with quietness than to have both hands full with vexation and travail.*

No wonder He said that it was in our best interest that He go away and the Comforter come. We live in a world of oppression. There is power in the oppressor's hand; but thank God, we do not have to live through it alone. We do not have to say, "Life is bad" or "I wish I were dead, and it would have been better if I had never lived." When the difficulties come in life, we can say that we have a Comforter who comes to us. Thank God that He does. He knows our sorrows.

In the eleventh chapter of John, the Lord Jesus stood at a grave and wept. In the nineteenth chapter of Luke, He stood beholding a city and wept. In the fifth chapter of Hebrews, He shed tears for a lost world. Jesus Christ is acquainted with weeping. God's Word says, *"Behold the tears."*

The Word of God says in Psalm 142:3-6,

> *When my spirit was overwhelmed within me, then thou knewest my path. In the way wherein I walked have they privily laid a snare for me. I looked on my*

right hand, and beheld, but there was no man that would know me: refuge failed me; no man cared for my soul. I cried unto thee, O LORD: I said, Thou art my refuge and my portion in the land of the living. Attend unto my cry; for I am brought very low: deliver me from my persecutors; for they are stronger than I.

Here we see oppression. As we give our considerations to life, we see that there are heartaches and tears. Life is not a bed of roses; it is filled with grief and trouble. We can struggle through it alone, or we can trust the Lord. We must make this decision. You may think no one knows what you are going through, but the Lord Jesus knows. He is the Comforter, and He will comfort you. He beholds the tears. His heart is moved. Just like He wept at the grave with loved ones, wept over the city of Jerusalem, and wept over this world, He beholds your tears and the Comforter will come to you. Just trust Him.

THE CONCLUSIONS

In Ecclesiastes 4:5 Solomon speaks of a fool. He said that the fool just folds his hands together and eats his own flesh. Then in verse six he said, *"Better is an handful with quietness, than both the hands full with travail and vexation of spirit."*

He reaches the conclusion that instead of trying to get everything you can and neglecting what you should not neglect, it would be better just to have one hand full with quietness than to have two hands full with travail and vexation of spirit. He then says in Ecclesiastes 4:7-8,

Then I returned, and I saw vanity under the sun. There is one alone, and there is not a second; yea, he hath neither child nor brother: yet is there no end of all his labour; neither is his eye satisfied with riches;

*neither saith he, For whom do I labour, and bereave my
soul of good? This is also vanity, yea, it is a sore travail.*

Are you trying to get both of your hands full? It would be better to
have one hand full with quietness than to have both hands full with
vexation and travail. What does this mean? It means that some people
who are wasting their families for some "brighter future" would be
better to settle for less and enjoy the moment. You may be working
very hard, going night and day. You may be unable to see your wife
and children as you want to, but you are planning for "someday." This
is wrong. One of these days, your wife will not even know you, and
your children will not want you around. You have never taken the time
to really know them. There is more to life than this.

Ecclesiastes 4:13 says, *"Better is a poor and wise child than an
old and foolish king."* Solomon was the king. He had everything he
desired, but he realized that he had been a fool. Some husbands and
wives are working so much that they barely cross paths during the
week. But why are they working? They may want a better car, a
better house, or more things. We need to realize that we are only
going to be young once, and we are only going to have our children
with us for a short time. We may be trying to get things for them, but
things alone will not satisfy.

I remember when I was growing up, my father would be gone for
six to eight weeks at a time. He always came home bearing gifts. He
did the best he could do. I said to my mother more than once, "You
know I'd rather have Daddy than to have these things he brings
home." If your children could get your attention, they would tell you
the same thing. They would rather have you.

I am not on some melancholy adventure down memory lane, but
I can only remember one time when my father passed a ball with me.
It stands out in my mind. He was not a very athletic man; he was
sickly. I remember one time that he got a friend to help him take us

fishing. I remember exactly where we went; I remember the whole day, just that one time. I can remember once we got in a foot race when I was a boy. I could take you to the very place; I know the yard in which we ran. The whole event stands out in my mind. Those times were so very few, and I said so often that I would rather have had my daddy than things.

I believe that the preacher here is speaking the truth when he says in Ecclesiastes 4:6, *"Better is an handful with quietness, than both the hands full with travail and vexation of spirit."* You may be better off not to move to a nicer neighborhood but rather give your children more of your life in the neighborhood you live in now. You may need to consider having a little less money to spend and being able to stay home with your wife and children and get acquainted with them instead of working and never seeing them while trying to provide more things for them. One of these days, you are going to

We have a Comforter. We have a Savior.

look back with regret. Even if you do the best you can, you are going to have some regrets, but if you are trying to get both hands full, you will have to say that it would have been better to have one hand full with quietness than both hands full with vexation and travail.

The Bible says in Proverbs 15:16-17, *"Better is little with the fear of the LORD than great treasure and trouble therewith. Better is a dinner of herbs where love is, than a stalled ox and hatred therewith."*

It would be better to have potato soup than to have the best steak in town, if there is no love in your home. The wind of the world blows and we are caught in it like a leaf. We go where the the wind blows. We want what the world wants. We do what the world does. We let the world tell us, "This is the way to live your life." God is saying to us, "Wait a minute! Your life is a vapor. It is soon gone."

Those people who are chasing the wind are going to say someday, "I would be better dead; it would be best if I'd never been born."

We do not have to live that way. We have a Comforter, the indwelling Holy Spirit, to guide us. We can live a different kind of life. We need to come to a conclusion about where our priorities are going to be placed. We need to decide that we are not going to put such a premium on possessions.

Many things happen in our lives that we cannot understand. We simply need to give them to God. I heard an old story about a farmer who passed by a brush pile on his farm. He saw that a little bird had started making a nest in the brush pile. He tore the nest from the brush pile. This seems like such a cruel thing to do. The next day, he walked by the same brush pile, and the little bird was back trying to make the nest again. Again, he destroyed the nest. The third day, believe it or not, he walked by the same brush pile, and the little bird was trying to make the nest for the third time. He tore the nest out of the brush pile again. The fourth day when he came by, he noticed that the same little bird had chosen a tree not far away in which to build her nest. That was the day the farmer burned the brush pile. He knew all along that he was going to burn the brush pile, but the little bird did not know it. What looked so violent to the little bird was really best because the farmer knew the future and the tiny bird did not.

> *It would be better to have potato soup than to have the best steak in town, if there is no love in your home.*

God knows the future, and He knows how we will be affected. There are times that God touches us and we weep. Then He comes to us in our weeping. He beholds our tears, and He helps us. He has an eternal purpose for this, and we need to trust Him. Some of us are weeping now. We do not have to weep alone. We simply need to trust the Lord Jesus Christ. Our God loves us, and He alone knows our future. Trust Him today!

"Better is a poor and a wise child than an old and foolish king, who will no more be admonished."

Ecclesiastes 4:13

Chapter Nine

A WISE CHILD OR A FOOLISH KING

 id you ever want to trade places with someone? Did you ever think that your life would be better if you were someone else or if you lived somewhere else? You will never find happiness and contentment with who you are as long as you want to be someone else.

The Bible says in Ecclesiastes 4:13, *"Better is a poor and wise child than an old and foolish king, who will no more be admonished."* Notice the expressions *"wise child"* and *"foolish king."*

I had no choice about who my mom and dad would be or where I would be born. I had no choice about my sex, male or female; that was God-determined. We need to be willing to accept the things that cannot be changed.

The writer of this passage was having trouble with life. Many people are having trouble with life. As a matter of fact, in Ecclesiastes 4:1-3 Solomon said,

> So I returned, and considered all the oppressions that are done under the sun: and behold the tears of such as were oppressed, and they had no comforter; and on the side of their oppressors there was power; but they had no comforter. Wherefore I praised the dead which are already dead more than the living which are yet alive. Yea, better is he than both they, which hath not yet been, who hath not seen the evil work that is done under the sun.

Solomon felt that it was bad to live, it would be better to die, and it would be best to have never been born. At this point in time, Solomon was a miserable man.

God has not designed life to be miserable. There are times when I am miserable, but I do not think that God designed my life to be this way. If that were the case, then why did the Lord Jesus say in John 10:10, *"I am come that they might have life, and that they might have it more abundantly"?* Why did Christ say that He had joy, and that we could be full of joy? There are certain things lacking in this life that cause us to have a longing for heaven, but life does not have to be bad. We do not have to wish we were dead or think that it would have been better if we had never been born.

The same man, King Solomon, said in verse eight of Ecclesiastes chapter four that there was no end to all his labor. He said that all he could see in front of him was work. He also said that his eye was not satisfied with riches. He could never stop working because he could never get enough. Then he said, *"Neither saith he, For whom do I labour?"* He did not even know why or for whom he was doing this. Life is not miserable except when it is lived away from God.

The apostle Paul wrote in I Corinthians 2:14, *"But the natural man receiveth not the things of the Spirit of God: for they are foolishness unto him: neither can he know them, because they are spiritually discerned."* The Bible says that a natural man does not receive the things of the Spirit of God. Not only does he fail to receive them, he says that they are foolish. They do not make sense to him. He cannot know them because they are spiritually discerned. In I Corinthians 3:1 Paul writes, *"And I, brethren, could not speak unto you as unto spiritual, but as unto carnal, even as unto babes in Christ."*

You will never find happiness and contentment with who you are as long as you want to be someone else.

We divide the world into saved people and lost people. By the word *saved,* we mean that someone has asked the Lord to forgive his sin and by faith has trusted Jesus Christ as his personal Savior. Have you done this? Do you believe that Jesus Christ is God, co-equal, eternally existent with God the Father and God the Holy Spirit? Do you believe that this same Christ came to earth, bled and died on Calvary's cross, was buried in a borrowed tomb, rose bodily from the dead and ascended on high? He ever lives to make intercession for us. If we ask Him to forgive our sin and receive Him as our Savior, He promises to save us. Was there a time in your life when you trusted in Christ and Christ alone for your salvation?

God divides the world into saved and lost, but the Christian world can be divided into those who are *spiritual* and those who are *carnal.* Unfortunately, many of God's children are carnal and do not have spiritual understanding. Many of God's children cannot discern between the things of this world and the things of the Lord. It is sad to be a child of God and yet not be a spiritual child of God. Not every Christian is spiritual. Not every Christian has done the things that are necessary to be able to think about and discern spiritual things. Are you a carnal Christian or a spiritual Christian? If you are a carnal Christian, then you are an unhappy Christian. You make wrong decisions that lead to wrong patterns in life. This can lead you down a road, sometimes for a long time, that can bring misery and pain. Every one of those pains, every bit of your misery, is a message from God. The Lord is using these things to remind you to stop and consider.

Possessions never bring happiness unless they are used for God.

In Ecclesiastes 4:9, we see some things that show good common sense. Solomon says that *"two are better than one."* The first reason for this is that they can receive a good reward for their labor. This is because two people can get more accomplished than one person. However, this is just common sense. An unsaved man could come up with this idea. The second reason is given in verses ten through twelve,

> *For if they fall, the one will lift up his fellow: but woe to him that is alone when he falleth; for he hath not another to help him up. Again, if two lie together, then they have heat: but how can one be warm alone? And if one prevail against him, two shall withstand him; and a threefold cord is not quickly broken.*

Much of what we say makes sense, but if we are living our lives with *only* what makes common sense; then we are carnal Christians. Is there a difference between these common sense things that anyone can know and being a spiritual person? There certainly is.

Sometimes we pride ourselves in what we know and how much we can do, and many of these things we can know and do without God. We need a deep re-examining to see if we are really dependent on the Lord.

Often the expression in Ecclesiastes 4:12 is used, *"A threefold cord is not quickly broken."* We use this expression for many things.

We use it in Christian education. We say that if we put the home, the church, and the school together, that threefold cord will help children. Again, Solomon is simply using common sense.

In Ecclesiastes 4:13 Solomon said, *"Better is a poor and a wise child than an old and foolish king, who will no more be admonished."* He realized that if he had a choice it would be better to be a poor and wise child that an old and foolish king. Have you ever heard anyone say, "I wish I could live that day over," or "I wish I could turn back the calendar," or "I wish I were young again"? I suppose that many people have had these thoughts race through their minds from time to time, but there is absolutely no sense in it because it is impossible. Some people are tormenting themselves by trying to be young again. Many older people try to look and act like teenagers.

HIS PALACE BECAME A PRISON

Solomon was on the throne of Israel, but he was a miserable man. There is a word in verse fourteen of chapter four that interests me. Solomon said, *"For out of prison he cometh to reign."* What does the word *"prison"* mean? If you study this particular word, you find that it refers to where this man lived. He said that he came out of prison. He was calling the palace a prison. He said, "I am the king of Israel. I came out of the palace, the son of a king, and now I am a king. My home is like a prison."

He was saying that he wanted to be king, and now he was, but instead of having the kingship, the kingship had him. The palace had become a prison. Sometimes we feel that we are in such a "fix" that we cannot get out. We feel as if our responsibilities are in control of us. We become bound, and we lose our joy.

Many people have chased after things. When they finally got what they wanted, they did not know what to do with it. Solomon said that he was king over Israel, but he felt as if he were in prison. He felt that he had started on top, but he had quickly tumbled downhill from there.

HIS POSSESSIONS POSSESSED HIM

If you make possessions your goal, someday your possessions will be reminders of how miserable you are. They will only serve to stare at you and remind you that chasing after their attainment did not satisfy you.

Most of us enjoy a quality of life far beyond what we grew up enjoying. We want that same quality for our children, but one of the things that helped us is not starting there. We want our children to start there. We want to try to save them from any pain or hurt. One of Solomon's problems was that he was born in the lap of luxury in the palace of the king. He had no place to go but down. We can learn a great lesson from the life of Solomon. Possessions never bring happiness unless they are used for God.

Solomon was the king of Israel; he had a great position. In Ecclesiastes 4:13-16 he wrote,

> *Better is a poor and a wise child than an old and foolish king, who will no more be admonished. For out of prison he cometh to reign; whereas also he that is born in his kingdom becometh poor. I considered all the living which walk under the sun, with the second child that shall stand up in his stead. There is no end of all the people, even of all that have been before them: they also that come after shall not rejoice in him. Surely this also is vanity and vexation of spirit.*

Solomon was a king. He had the position, but when he looked at life, he said that all was vanity. You may have a position, but some days you wish you were somewhere down the line from where you are because of all the expectations and responsibilities that are placed on your position. It is a place of misery unless it is given to God. If it is not used for God, you can see only one side of it. You see all the expectations, responsibilities, and the labor that never ends. You see this as opposed to seeing that God put you in that place of influence so you can use that position for Him and for His glory. The Lord places us in positions of influence that can be used for His honor and glory. Possessions will never bring happiness unless they are used for God, and a position will never bring happiness unless it is used for God.

HIS POPULARITY WAS WITHOUT PRAISE TO GOD

The king said in Ecclesiastes 4:16, *"There is no end of all the people, even of all that have been before them: they also that come after shall not rejoice in him. Surely this also is vanity and vexation of spirit."*

If people recognize your name and know who you are, what does it really matter? The high visibility that people strive for will never bring happiness unless it is given to God and used for God. Every person who has people call on him because of his visibility or "popularity" will be miserable if he does not realize that this comes with accountability to God.

Why do you think that God let you be a boss, a leader, or a teacher? Why do you think God made your name stand out above other names? You will be a miserable person if you do not use this visibility for Him and for His glory. Life becomes such a burden unless we see that God has given us influence that we can use for His glory.

Solomon said that apart from God and spiritual mindedness, everything under the sun is vanity. It is all empty. He had gold and silver; he may have been the wealthiest man who ever lived. He had the highest position in the land. He was the most popular person on earth. However, he said that with all his possessions, position, and popularity, he was miserable, and his life was empty and vain.

Unless your life is lived and used for God, the things that are great blessings become great curses. Solomon said that he would rather be a poor child out playing somewhere that no one knew than to be the king of Israel and be such a foolish man.

There is a word in verse thirteen that I think is the key to understanding this. *"Better is a poor and wise child than an old and foolish king, who will no more be admonished."* He said the thing about being a child is that children are teachable. He realized that, as an old and foolish king, he would not be *"admonished."* He was no longer teachable. Are you at the place in life where you cannot be taught?

The Lord Jesus concluded the Sermon on the Mount with a story in Matthew 7:24-29,

> *Therefore whosoever heareth these sayings of mine, and doeth them, I will liken him unto a wise man which built his house upon a rock: and the rain descended, and the floods came, and the winds blew, and beat upon that house; and it fell not: for it was founded upon a rock. And every one that heareth these sayings of mine, and doeth them not, shall be likened unto a foolish man, which built his house upon the sand: and the rain descended, and the floods came, and the winds blew, and beat upon that house; and it fell: and great was the fall of it. And it came to pass, when Jesus had ended these sayings, the people were astonished at his doctrine: for he taught them as one having authority, and not as the scribes.*

Solomon said that he would rather be a wise child than a foolish king. The foolish king is foolish because he is no longer *admonished*. He will not receive admonition or be taught. The Lord

Jesus said that we are foolish if we hear and do not obey. Christ said that we are wise if we hear and obey.

Are you still teachable? Children are teachable. They are tender, truthful, and teachable. Solomon says that a foolish king will not be admonished, but a wise child will.

My wife and I were talking one evening about how happy we are that we have been able to be together all of these years and be in the work of the Lord. We are grateful. Then we began thinking about how we sometimes take things for granted. We get the idea that certain things should come our way, that certain things belong to us.

Do you know what the Bible calls this? The Bible calls this the sin of presumption. In Psalm 19, there are *"secret faults,"* *"presumptuous sins,"* and *"the great transgression."* The secret sin must be dealt with, then the presumptuous sin must be dealt with so that we never get to the place where we have a great transgression.

I must remind myself that I am nothing without the Lord and that I owe the Lord Jesus everything. If my life were cut off at this moment, He has been better to me than I ever deserved. I deserve nothing but hell. May God bring us back to reality, and may He help us to remain teachable.

I have been in the ministry since July of 1967. If I am not careful, I may begin to think that I know everything. I may think that I have enough in the bank of knowledge to draw from for the rest of my life. God will not allow you or me to live without letting us know that we need to trust Him and lean on Him each day.

"Keep thy foot when thou goest to the house of God, and be more ready to hear, than to give the sacrifice of fools: for they consider not that they do evil."

Ecclesiastes 5:1

Chapter Ten

BE READY TO HEAR

hink what God could tell us and how it could affect our lives for good if we would simply hear Him. God speaks to us through His Word. He also speaks to us through circumstances. Some of us have had things happen in our lives that have made us ready to listen and to hear God. A third way He speaks to us is through other Christians. It is the desire of our God to speak to us, and we need to be ready to hear. The Word of God says in Ecclesiastes 5:1-7,

> *Keep thy foot when thou goest to the house of God, and be more ready to hear, than to give the sacrifice of fools: for they consider not that they do evil. Be not rash with thy mouth, and let not thine heart be hasty to utter any thing before God: for God is in heaven, and thou upon earth: therefore*

let thy words be few. For a dream cometh through the multitude of business; and a fool's voice is known by multitude of words. When thou vowest a vow unto God, defer not to pay it; for he hath no pleasure in fools: pay that which thou hast vowed. Better is it that thou shouldest not vow, than that thou shouldest vow and not pay. Suffer not thy mouth to cause thy flesh to sin; neither say thou before the angel, that it was an error: wherefore should God be angry at thy voice, and destroy the work of thine hands? For in the multitude of dreams and many words there are also divers vanities: but fear thou God.

This is a passage that should be read a number of times. I believe that after reading it several times, you will begin to understand the message of the passage. Notice the words in the first verse, *"ready to hear."*

Are you ready to hear? Through the providence of God, He is always working in our lives to make us ready to hear. I sometimes hear parents say concerning a child, "I have tried and tried to tell him, but he just won't listen." When he gets ready to hear, he will.

Two old farmers decided that they would trade mules. One told the other that he had the finest mule in the country and that it could do more work than any other mule he had ever seen. So the farmer traded for the mule and took it into the field to plow, but the mule would not move. They were not far from the barn, and about that time the other farmer appeared on the scene. The first farmer said, "This mule you traded me, that is supposed to be such a hard worker, will not do a thing." The farmer who traded the mule to the fellow walked into the barn, got a great big two-by-four, hit the mule in the side of the head, and the mule fell to the ground. As the mule was lying on the ground, the farmer whispered to the mule, "Now, get up and plow." Sure enough, the mule got up and started plowing. The farmer who struck the mule said, "You just have to make him ready to listen."

God works overtime getting some of us ready to hear. It is not that He has nothing to say. He has much to say, but we are not ready to hear Him.

There is a beautiful connection in this verse between our hearing and our going to the house of God. Ecclesiastes 5:1 says, *"Keep thy foot when thou goest to the house of God, and be more ready to hear, than to give the sacrifice of fools: for they consider not that they do evil."* Solomon spoke about going up to the temple. All kinds of activities take place in churches that really have nothing to do with hearing the Word of God. Many people attend church, but they do not hear. God says that when we go to the house of God, we are to be ready to hear.

Our Lord will always enable us to do what He has led us to attempt for Him.

In Matthew chapter seventeen, we read the account of the transfiguration of the Lord Jesus. What an exciting event this was as Christ went up into a high mountain to be transfigured into the glorious likeness that He shall come in some day. Peter, James, and John were able to make the trip up into that high mountain with Him. They saw Him transfigured. Christ stood there in His glory, and Moses and Elijah came and stood beside Him. Moses represents all those who have died in the Lord whose bodies have been buried and are awaiting the resurrection. Elijah represents the group of people who will never die and will be alive when the Lord Jesus comes again in His glory. The Bible says in Matthew 17:1-5,

> *And after six days Jesus taketh Peter, James, and John his brother, and bringeth them up into an high mountain apart, and was transfigured before them: and his face did shine as the sun, and his raiment was white as the light. And, behold, there appeared unto*

> *them Moses and Elias talking with him. Then*
> *answered Peter, and said unto Jesus, Lord, it is good*
> *for us to be here: if thou wilt, let us make here three*
> *tabernacles; one for thee, and one for Moses, and one*
> *for Elias. While he yet spake, behold, a bright cloud*
> *overshadowed them: and behold a voice out of the*
> *cloud, which said, This is my beloved Son, in whom I*
> *am well pleased; hear ye him.*

This was a very exciting time. The Lord Jesus was in His glory. Moses and Elijah were there. That would excite anyone. Peter felt that it was so wonderful there that he did not ever want to go back down to the valley. He wanted to stay on this wonderful "mountain-top" experience. He got so excited that he said, *"Let us make here three tabernacles; one for thee, one for Moses, and one for Elias."* Then God spoke from heaven and said, *"This is my beloved Son, in whom I am well pleased; hear ye him."* Listen to the Lord Jesus Christ; let Him speak to you. It is time to hear from the Lord.

In James 1:19 the Bible says, *"Wherefore, my beloved brethren, let every man be swift to hear, slow to speak, slow to wrath."* I want to ask you a personal question, "Are you ready to hear?"

THE VIEW GOD HAS OF OUR LIVES

Ecclesiastes 5:2 says, *"Be not rash with thy mouth, and let not thine heart be hasty to utter any thing before God: for God is in heaven, and thou upon earth: therefore let thy words be few."* Notice the expression, *"for God is in heaven."* Solomon was talking about the view that God has of things. When we come to the house of God, God is in heaven. You may say that God dwells in the heart of every believer. He certainly does, but the Bible says that God is in heaven.

To illustrate to us that God is in heaven and that He sees everything, the Bible says in Proverbs 15:3, *"The eyes of the LORD are in every place, beholding the evil and the good."* The view God has of your life is not the view that you have of your life. The perspective that God has of your life is not the perspective that you have of your life.

After I had conducted a wedding, a lady said to me, "I wish I had your perspective and your view of things." She said, "I would have given anything to be able to see the faces of those young people." She had in mind, of course, that the bride and groom were facing me and that I saw expressions on their faces that she was not able to witness.

In the view that God has of our lives, He sees everything. Not only does He see us, He sees all the circumstances surrounding us. He sees the things that have come into our lives and the things that are coming to our lives. The view that God has is something we need to consider. God is in heaven. He sees the whole picture; not part of it, not one day or one moment of it. He knows what we need. The Lord uses ministers who speak the truth of God's Word to give us messages that provide direction for our lives.

THE VOW WE MAKE TO GOD

In this passage, we are following a natural progression. We are going up to the house of God. God is going to speak. God has a view of the whole picture, and He speaks. When He speaks, we make vows to Him. We commit certain things to Him that we are going to do. The Bible says in Ecclesiastes 5:4-5, *"When thou vowest a vow unto God, defer not to pay it; for he hath no pleasure in fools: pay that which thou hast vowed. Better is it that thou shouldest not vow, than that thou shouldest vow and not pay."*

Some people take their vows lightly. You may say, "Oh, years ago in church, I made some kind of statement to the Lord. Somewhere as a boy I said, 'Yes God, I'll follow You.' Oh, that was years ago." Many things may have taken place in your life since then, but God still remembers the vow that you made. The Bible says, *"Better is it that thou shouldest not vow, than that thou shouldest vow and not pay."*

The only thing we have to do to waste our lives is to do nothing. People say, "Well, I'm not out doing bad things." But all we must do to throw our lives away is to simply drift through life. We need to be making some vows to God that bring the right kind of commitment and discipline to our lives.

> *When we go to the house of God, we are to be ready to hear.*

This is the first generation to ever have the ability and technology to track all the people on the earth. This is the first generation to ever have the ability to communicate globally with people simultaneously. This is the first generation with the ability to eliminate or control world-wide currencies. This is the first generation with the ability to monitor the movement of people electronically. This is the first generation with the ability to control or monitor all buying and all selling by computers. Surely we realize that if man can stay in contact with man in such a way, that God is able to keep up with each of us.

God spoke to my heart when someone explained to me that Jesus Christ came from heaven to bleed and die for my sin. He was buried and rose from the dead. This person said to me, "Will you ask the Lord Jesus to forgive your sin and by faith receive Him as your Savior?" I prayed and asked Him to forgive my sin, and I received Jesus Christ into my life as my personal Savior. I was born again. I promised God that I would live all my life for Him. I made a vow to God. Have you made that vow to God?

God directed my life and called me to preach. I surrendered to His call, and I made a vow to God that I would be a preacher of the gospel. Have you made a vow to God that you will be what He desires for you to be?

When God gave me a wife, I made a vow to God to have a Christian home. Have you made that vow to God? When God gave me children, I made a vow to God to teach those children the truth of the Word of God. There is a world of difference between parental participation and God-given parental responsibility. It is one thing for a man to say that he is going to attend the ball games and other activities with his children; it is another thing entirely to say that he has a holy obligation to God to teach those children the truth. Have you made that vow to God?

The Bible says that when we go up to the house of God, we should be ready to hear. God has a view of our lives that no one else has, and He speaks to us. When He speaks, we make vows to Him concerning what He leads us to do. You may think that you are afraid to make a vow. Do not be afraid. There is no one in this world so interested in your life as the Lord. There is no one in this world that cares so much about you as God does. It is right to make vows to the Lord.

THE VICTORY WE CAN HAVE

This victory is very simple. The Bible says in Ecclesiastes 5:6, *"Suffer not thy mouth to cause thy flesh to sin..."* What does this mean? Do not talk yourself out of what you said you were going to do. If you said you were going to do something, ask the Lord to help you and do not talk yourself out of it. Do not let your mouth cause your flesh to sin. He continues, *"...neither say thou before the angel, that it was an error."*

Who is this angel? I have a surprise for you; the angel is the preacher, God's messenger. If you do not believe this, go to the book of Revelation chapters two and three and read about *"the angel of the church."* The Bible says not to go to the angel and say that your vow was an error. The word *angel* means "messenger." Do not go to the messenger God used to speak to you and say, "Wait a minute. I am backing out of this thing. It is not for me." Do not go to the messenger and talk like that. Have you recognized God's messengers in your life? Have you recognized the places where you have met God and He has spoken to you?

I love it when I attend a church service or when I am alone with God and the Lord gets my attention, speaks to me, and leads me to do something. This helps me to know that God is still very interested in my life. The view that God has is not like our view; He is in heaven. There are vows that we make to Him. The victory we can have is very simple; it is by continuing with what we have said we are going to do. This is the simplest formula to victory. When I feel like giving up and turning around, I must stay with what I said I was going to do as the Lord led me. Ecclesiastes 5:6-7 says,

> *Suffer not thy mouth to cause thy flesh to sin; neither say thou before the angel, that it was an error: wherefore should God be angry at thy voice, and destroy the work of thine hands? For in the multitude of dreams and many words there are also divers vanities: but fear thou God.*

God simply says not to let your mouth talk you out of keeping your vow. Do not run to the messenger and try to back out of something that God has led you to do. Instead of trying to back out of it, ask the Lord to help you to do it. What has God spoken to you about? What has He led you to do? Go further into it. Ask the Lord to help you. Our Lord will always enable us to do what He has led us to attempt for Him.

Then the Lord warns us again when He says, *"For in the multitude of dreams and many words there are also divers vanities..."*

If you are not careful, you will get with the wrong crowd and in the wrong environment, and people will start giving you vain, empty ideas for your life. As you hear all the empty noise, you will get away from what God has led you to do.

Then God's Word says, *"...but fear thou God."* When we come to the conclusion about our lives, we must be sure we are doing what the Lord wants us to do. How many of us have needed advice lately? Some people have much advice to give, and most of it is not to be heeded. When we start wanting to know direction or advice, we are apt to get a great amount of it. In all of it, we must be careful; because in the end, the only thing that matters is fearing God and doing what He wants us to do.

The view God has of your life is not the view that you have of your life.

A young man once came to me seeking counsel. He was graduating from college and he told me that he had more than one opportunity to go somewhere to serve the Lord. I told him that I had several churches contact me at one time, and every one of them spoke as if they knew for sure that it was God's will for me to be their pastor. Each church said, "We're just sure that God wants you to be our pastor." It is thrilling that someone wants you, but what are we going to do with all these ideas? How are we going to know what it is that God is saying? Are you ready to hear? When you fear God, you are going to know His voice. God's Word says, *"But fear thou God."*

Dr. Lee Roberson often says, "When in doubt, don't." Why jump into some great decision if you are in doubt about it? I am not talking about doubting your inability or doubting your lack of wisdom. I am talking about not knowing for sure what God wants. If you do not know what God wants, just sit still. When you do know, and you have said, "Lord, I'll do it," then follow God with all of your heart. Be ready to hear.

How many of us know that we have been in church at one time or another and God has spoken to us? We did not hear an audible voice. The Lord may have used a preacher's voice, but we definitely received leading from the Lord. It was an impression God gave our spirit, and God let us know what we were to do, where we were to go, or the decision we were to make. We should come to every meeting expecting God to speak to us. We should live every day expecting God to speak to us. When He speaks, we should be ready to hear and obey.

"Every man also to whom God hath given riches and wealth, and hath given him power to eat thereof, and to take his portion, and to rejoice in his labour; this is the gift of God. For he shall not much remember the days of his life; because God answereth him in the joy of his heart."

Ecclesiastes 5:19-20

Chapter
Eleven

THE SUNNY
SIDE OF LIFE

or years I signed every letter that I wrote with a little footnote that said, "Stay on the sunny side of life." At some point in time, I stopped writing this note, but the sad thing is that too often I have stopped living it. Some things are very difficult for us to discuss because we are not good at doing them.

Abraham Lincoln said that until you are forty years old, God is responsible for the way you look. He said that after forty, you are responsible for the way you look. Of course he meant that the experiences of life and the way we respond to them begin to show on our countenance. After a certain point in life, our countenance displays what we think about life. I do not know if Mr. Lincoln was right or not, but at least I understand the point.

There is a very interesting story of George Muller, the preacher in England of more than a century ago who cared for hundreds of orphans. Mr. Muller was constantly faced with tremendous needs in caring for the orphaned children. A farmer who had passed George Muller on the road one day said, "I was going up Ashley Hill one morning, when I met George Muller walking toward the city. Had I not known him, I should have said he was a gentleman of leisure, and without a care. So quietly did he walk, and so peaceful and stately was his demeanor. The Twenty-third Psalm was written in his face." Though Muller carried great responsibility and heavy burdens, he was living on the sunny side of life. What side of life are you living on?

As we consider Ecclesiastes chapter five, verses eight to twenty, there are two expressions in this passage I would like for us to notice. The first is in verse twenty, *"the joy of his heart."* The second is in verse seventeen, where we find *"his days also he eateth in darkness."* Let us consider living on the "sunny side" of life.

THE WRONG SIDE

There is a wrong side to life. The Bible says in Ecclesiastes 5:8, *"If thou seest the oppression of the poor, and violent perverting of judgment and justice in a province, marvel not at the matter: for he that is higher than the highest regardeth; and there be higher than they."*

God says that you may see oppression of the poor and violent perverting of judgment. As a matter of fact, we see it all around us. I read in the newspaper once about a teenage boy in Union, Kentucky, who woke up at five o'clock in the morning, took a gun, walked into his parents' bedroom, and shot and killed his mother and father. He then walked into his sisters' bedroom and killed them. The newspaper said that there was surely something wrong with this boy. I agree! They said that he had been dressing in black and had been warned about carrying a gun to school. He talked about how much fun it would be to kill people.

Stories like this are shocking, but not as shocking as they once were. Although I am sure that the people in that boy's hometown were very shocked, we hear so much today that we are not as shocked as we once were. Our world is full of oppression and perversion. We are living in a day when many people call right wrong and wrong right; good evil and evil good. They call light darkness and darkness light. God's Word says in Isaiah 5:20, *"Woe unto them that call evil good, and good evil; that put darkness for light, and light for darkness; that put bitter for sweet, and sweet for bitter!"* People who believe and preach the Bible and stand for what is right are called the enemies of the unbelieving world. We are living in a world that has gone wrong.

> *It would be better for your children to be left a godly heritage than money in the bank.*

When I was a boy, my folks would let me go out in the morning, and they would only make sure I checked in before dark. Today, parents want to hold a child tightly by the arm or hand no matter where they are. I can remember going shopping with my mother and she would say, "The restroom is back in the corner of the store. I will wait for you here near the dresses." Parents cannot do that today. No one does that today if he is in his right mind. Why? Because we are living in a world that has gone wrong.

We know what is wrong. We can point out what is wrong. We see the oppression and the violent perverting of judgment. I could give you illustration after illustration, but I do not think it is necessary. The point is proven each day we live. We are already very much aware that we are living in this kind of world.

There is a wrong side of life. The Bible says in Ecclesiastes 5:10-11, *"He that loveth silver shall not be satisfied with silver..."* This is part of the wrong side of life. People think that just a little more, or maybe much more, will make them happy. The Bible says that if one loves silver or material things, he is going to find that these things will never satisfy. This is part of the wrong side of life.

The passage continues, *"..nor he that loveth abundance with increase: this is also vanity. When goods increase, they are increased that eat them: and what good is there to the owners thereof, saving the beholding of them with their eyes?"*

When this passage is properly understood, it reminds us of the man who said that when he made one hundred dollars a week, he could hardly make ends meet; and now that he makes one thousand dollars a week, he still can hardly make ends meet. You will never find what you are looking for in things. People who are trying to find satisfaction in things are on the wrong side of life.

The Bible says in Ecclesiastes 5:12, *"The sleep of a labouring man is sweet, whether he eat little or much: but the abundance of the rich will not suffer him to sleep."* It is hard to imagine what some people would give for one good night's rest, and they cannot get that one good night's sleep.

Ecclesiastes 5:13-14 says, *"There is a sore evil which I have seen under the sun, namely, riches kept for the owners thereof to their hurt. But those riches perish by evil travail: and he begetteth a son, and there is nothing in his hand."* Many people say, "I am working. I am earning. I am living. I am saving. I am laying up treasure, and I'm going to leave it all to my children." This is not what the Bible teaches we should do. The Bible says that if you live with the wrong motive and teach your children by example to live that way, when you die you may leave a huge sum of money, but the truth of the matter is that you are leaving them nothing. It would be better for your children to be left a godly heritage than money in the bank.

THE RIGHT SIDE

In Ecclesiastes 5:15-16 the Bible says, *"As he came forth of his mother's womb, naked shall he return to go as he came, and shall take nothing of his labour, which he may carry away in his hand. And this also is a sore evil, that in all points as he came, so shall he go: and what profit hath he that hath laboured for the wind?"*

On the right side of life, we understand that we start from our mother's womb naked and we shall return as we came, with nothing but our naked souls to meet God. Living on the right side of life is understanding that we came into this world with nothing, and we will go out with nothing. We are going to meet God someday; and while we are here, we need to trust the Lord Jesus Christ as our personal Savior, live for the Lord, obey the Lord, and do what is right before Him. This is the right side of life.

In I Timothy 6:6-7 the Bible says, *"But godliness with contentment is great gain. For we brought nothing into this world, and it is certain we can carry nothing out."* Living on the right side of life involves understanding the principle of godliness with contentment. I know I am right about the Bible because it is the Word of God. When the Bible says that we are going out to meet God with nothing but our naked souls, it is true because the Bible says it.

I know I am right about heaven and hell. I know I am right because the Bible says that there is a real hell from which the souls of men must be saved, and there is a real heaven. Jesus Christ came from heaven to bleed and die on the cross and to pay our sin debt so that if we ask Him to forgive our sin and receive Him as our Savior, we do not have to die and go to hell. We can go to heaven when we die by trusting Christ as Savior. I know I am right about this. This is the right side.

Ecclesiastes 5:17 says, *"All his days also he eateth in darkness, and he hath much sorrow and wrath with his sickness."* We understand that life is filled with sorrow. The Bible says in Job 14:1, *"Man that is born of a woman is of few days, and full of trouble."* We must come to grips with this. We know that living on the wrong side of life is living in this sin-cursed world and dying without Christ. Living on the right side is trusting Jesus Christ as Savior and recognizing that we came into this world with nothing and we are going out with nothing.

The point is that there is a wrong side and a right side to life. However, I am deeply concerned that some of us who know the wrong side and the right side have missed the "sunny side" entirely. This is where we have gone astray.

THE BRIGHT SIDE

So many of us who are on the right side are not on the bright side. So many of us have all of our facts straight and can say, "Yes, I know what I believe is true. I stand strong on the Word of God." This is right, but there are many of us who are right whose lives are not bright. Our lives do not show forth the light of Jesus Christ.

I have certain convictions about how God's people should live, how they should behave, and how they should talk. I get these convictions from the Bible. I have an understanding of what is happening in the world because God has told us about His program. He told us that Jesus Christ is coming again, and that evil men and seducers shall wax worse and worse.

Frankly, the world is not going to get any better; it is going to get worse. It may appear to be better, but it is really worse. Men may know how to dress up their evil to make it more beautiful, but it is really worse because the Bible says in II Timothy 3:13 that *"evil men and seducers shall wax worse and worse."* The longer we live, the worse this world becomes. We know this because the Bible teaches it.

It is very difficult when living in a wrong world, even having been taught right doctrine, not to be overcome by feelings that things are so bad around us. It seems very difficult to live a bright Christian life. One of the chief things that keeps lost people from coming to Christ is not our lack of being right; it is our lack of being bright as Christians. We are the light, and the light must shine. To think about all the wicked things that are happening in this world is sometimes overwhelming, but we must be hopeful. Our Lord has designed the Christian life to be joyful.

Most of the time we do not realize how much we have until it is irretrievably gone.

We see in the Gospel according to John, chapter fifteen, the way we should live as Christians. The Lord Jesus said in John 15:11, *"These things have I spoken unto you, that my joy might remain in you, and that your joy might be full."* Some of the very best people I know need to join with me in saying that we know we are right, but we have failed to be bright. I desire that my *"joy might be full."*

There is a wrong side, and we find most of the world living on the wrong side. There is a right side, but there is also a bright side. People who are right also need to be bright, shining lights for Jesus Christ. Please understand that these thoughts are not simply about positive thinking; this is a message on the victorious life we have in the Lord Jesus Christ. We have so much to be bright about; but we stay so upset about what is wrong that we lose sight of Christ.

You may say, "I know I am right." I commend you. God bless you; I would not want you to believe anything else, but we need to be bright also. We need to have lives filled with the joy of the Lord.

In Ecclesiastes 5:18 the Bible says, *"Behold that which I have seen: it is good and comely for one to eat and to drink, and to enjoy the good of all his labour that he taketh under the sun all the days of his life, which God giveth him: for it is his portion."*

We have the idea that we can only enjoy what our labor can produce. In other words, I may think that I cannot enjoy speaking for Christ; I can only enjoy it if something results from my speaking. Can I not learn to enjoy studying? Can I not learn to enjoy delivering the message? Can I not enjoy talking about the Lord Jesus and lifting Him up? Certainly I can! We must learn to enjoy the journey just as we hope to enjoy our destination.

People may say, "With what I can do with my money, I can have joy." Wait a minute. What about what you did to get the money? We have developed the philosophy that we cannot enjoy anything until the end. The truth of the matter is that the end never proves to be as joyous as we thought it would be, so we are never as happy as we should be.

Parents may say, "When I get these kids raised–when I finally get them out of the house, and get them through school–I will be happy." Then you go into an empty house and you cry, and go into their rooms, and sit on their beds and wonder where the years have gone. God meant for us to enjoy the journey. The Bible says very plainly in verse eighteen, *"to enjoy the good of all his labour."* This speaks of living on the bright side of life. We must learn to enjoy the journey. It will be over before we know it.

Notice the expression in Ecclesiastes 5:18, *"which God giveth him."* Our lives are gifts from God. This causes me to think about what Dr. Vance Havner said in my presence after the death of his wife. He said, "What I would give for one more day with her! It could even be a sick day when all I would do is sit by her bedside." Most of the time we do not realize how much we have until it is irretrievably gone. Think of life without your precious loved ones. God says that it will help us live the bright life if we realize that life is a gift from God.

In Ecclesiastes 5:19 the Bible says, *"Every man also to whom God hath given riches and wealth, and hath given him power to eat thereof, and to take his portion, and to rejoice in his labour; this is the gift of God."* Notice the expression, *"this is the gift of God."* You may say that you have worked hard and done well for yourself. Where did you get your mind, your ability, and your opportunity? These are gifts from God.

The Bible continues in Ecclesiastes 5:20, *"For he shall not much remember the days of his life; because God answereth him in the joy of his heart."* Notice the expression *"the joy of his heart."* What does this mean? It means that life will not seem to that person like some strenuous thing that he must grind his way through. It means that life can be joyous when we view it as a gift from God.

In the Old Testament, we read a story about Jacob. He went to Uncle Laban and he found a girl by the name of Rachel. She was beautiful to behold, and he loved her. He ended up working seven years for her, and he was given her sister instead of her. He had to work seven more years to get Rachel. The Bible says in Genesis 29:20, *"And Jacob served seven years for Rachel; and they seemed unto him but a few days, for the love he had to her."*

Seven years seemed like just a few days because he loved her so much. With that in mind, look at the last verse of Ecclesiastes chapter five again, *"For he shall not much remember the days of his life; because God answereth him in the joy of his heart."*

Could it be that God has a Christian life that is so wonderful, and filled with such joy, that at the end of our journey we could say, "I don't even remember the days, God has put such joy in my heart. It seems like no time."

Recall very carefully and prayerfully what Charles Spurgeon said in one of his sermons,

I, from my calling, have many scores of times seen saints in their last hours. This is the witness I put on record–the very happiest persons I have ever met with have been departing believers.

I have not met at weddings, nor at jubilee feasts, nor in moments of singular prosperity, such joyful persons as I have seen amid weakness and pain upon their dying beds. The only sons of men for whom I have felt any envy have been dying members of this very church, whose hands I have grasped in their passing away.

Almost without any exception I have seen in them holy delight and triumph; and deep peace, exhibited in a calm and deliberate readiness to enter into the presence of their God. They have been as ready for the eternal world as they would have been to rise from their beds and return to their daily callings on the Monday morning. 'The peace of God, which passeth all understanding' has kept their hearts and minds even when the joy of the Lord has not lifted them into transports or ecstasies. Saintly death-beds are grand evidences of Christianity.

My precious wife and I have been serving the Lord together since July of 1967. Sometimes it seems like a moment. I want to know what the wrong side is, and I do not want to be on the wrong side. I also want to have a good understanding of the right side, knowing that I have trusted the Lord Jesus as my Savior. But, I want to do a better job of learning to enjoy my labor because it is a gift from God. I want to do a better job of living on the bright side and demonstrate by the life I live that there truly is joy in knowing Jesus Christ.

*"For who knoweth what is good for man
in this life, all the days of his vain life
which he spendeth as a shadow? for who
can tell a man what shall be after
him under the sun?"*

Ecclesiastes 6:12

Chapter Twelve

WHO COMES BEFORE WHAT

he book of Ecclesiastes is about living life to the fullest. The key to understanding this message about life is understanding the expression *"under the sun,"* which means "on the earth, apart from God; living as if there is no God." As long as we live under the sun, as if there is no God, we will never be able to live life to the fullest.

Some people say they are Christians, but they live no differently than those without God. There are *professing* atheists who say, "I believe there is no God," and there are *practicing* atheists, those who say with their lips that there is a God but live their lives as if there is no God.

The sixth chapter of the book of Ecclesiastes marks a turning point in this sermon about life. The preacher is King Solomon, son of David. Solomon was the most privileged man to ever live.

The Bible says in Ecclesiastes 6:1-12,

> *There is an evil which I have seen under the sun, and it is common among men: a man to whom God hath given riches, wealth, and honour, so that he wanteth nothing for his soul of all that he desireth, yet God giveth him not power to eat thereof, but a stranger eateth it: this is vanity, and it is an evil disease. If a man beget an hundred children, and live many years, so that the days of his years be many, and his soul be not filled with good, and also that he have no burial; I say, that an untimely birth is better than he. For he cometh in with vanity, and departeth in darkness, and his name shall be covered with darkness. Moreover he hath not seen the sun, nor known any thing: this hath more rest than the other. Yea, though he live a thousand years twice told, yet hath he seen no good: do not all go to one place? All the labour of man is for his mouth, and yet the appetite is not filled. For what hath the wise more than the fool? what hath the poor, that knoweth to walk before the living? Better is the sight of the eyes than the wandering of the desire: this is also vanity and vexation of spirit. That which hath been is named already, and it is known that it is man: neither may he contend with him that is mightier than he. Seeing there be many things that increase vanity, what is man the better? For who knoweth what is good for man in this life, all the days of his vain life which he spendeth as a shadow? for who can tell a man what shall be after him under the sun?*

Notice the word *"who"* and the word *"what"* in the last verse of Ecclesiastes chapter six. In the latter part of this verse, the words *"who"* and *"what"* are mentioned again. God's Word says, *"For who knoweth what is good for man in this life? all the days of his vain life which he spendeth as a shadow? for who can tell a man what shall be after him under the sun?"*

The message is very simple, yet I think it is the key to life. The message is "Who Comes Before What." As you look at your Bible, you will see this for yourself. The emphasis of this chapter in the Bible is not about death and eternity; it is about life.

Who comes before *what*. What do I mean by this? I have given my life to try to help people because God has called me to do this. He did not drag me into it. He put a desire in my heart to do it. The miracle of the ministry is not that I am in

> *Every ability and opportunity is a liability until it is yielded to God.*

it, but that I want to be in it. God has placed in my heart a desire to serve Him. I have tried these many years to counsel people and give them advice from the Word of God about what they should do. I have made many mistakes because I have paid too much attention to *what* people should do and not enough attention to *Who* can tell them what they should do.

When young people are graduating from high school or college, they are often asked, *"What* are you going to do with your life?" It becomes frustrating at times to think, "I don't know what I'm going to do with my life." We need to remind them that there is a God in heaven who can tell them what He wants them to do with their lives.

God may allow you to continue to do the same thing you are presently doing. The point is that we should not be doing what we are doing without knowing it is what God wants us to do. Knowing who God is, coming into His presence and seeking Him are the things we should do first; then, God will direct us. *Who* comes before *what*.

GOD BRINGS US TO A PERSON, NOT A PLACE

In Exodus 19:4, God spoke to Moses about bringing the children of Israel out of Egyptian bondage and taking them into the Promised Land. Here we find a tremendous thought. As we read this verse, we see that God does not call us to a place or to some geographical location. This is a very common mistake all of us make. Some of you may be in an unlikely place. Think beyond the place. It is not a place to which God has called you, it is a Person to whom God has called you.

The Bible says in Exodus 19:4, *"Ye have seen what I did unto the Egyptians..."* We have read about how the Lord broke the yoke of Egyptian bondage after the plagues came to Egypt. God delivered His people. He brought them through the Red Sea and then closed the sea upon the Egyptians.

The only rest I find in my life is when I am trusting the Lord. There is a sweet peace and rest in faith.

Exodus 19:4 continues, *"...and how I bare you on eagles' wings, and brought you unto myself."* The Lord said He brought them unto Himself, not unto a place. God brought me to where I presently serve to bring me closer to Him. Wherever you are and whatever you are doing, the circumstance is not nearly as important as we have made it to be. The surrounding is not nearly as important as we have made it to be. God is working in each of our lives to bring us closer to Him.

Many of God's children, on the front side of suffering, have said, "I would never want to go through such a thing. May God spare me from it!" But on the other side of the suffering, they say, "Thank God I went through this trial, because it changed my life. The Lord spoke to me through it. I learned something about the Lord that I never knew before I went through this. It caused me to draw closer to God."

WHAT WE DO IS NOT AS IMPORTANT AS WHO GOD IS

We must get the *who* before the *what*. In Psalm 37:3-4 the Bible says, *"Trust in the LORD, and do good; so shalt thou dwell in the land, and verily thou shalt be fed. Delight thyself also in the LORD; and he shall give thee the desires of thine heart."*

God's Word says, *"Delight thyself also in the LORD,"* then, *"He shall give thee the desires of thine heart."* Who He is comes before what we desire. The Bible says in Psalm 37:5, *"Commit thy way unto the LORD; trust also in him; and he shall bring it to pass."* Again, who comes before what.

In Proverbs 3:5-6 the Bible says, *"Trust in the LORD with all thine heart; and lean not unto thine own understanding. In all thy ways acknowledge him, and he shall direct thy paths."*

Let us be honest with one another. What we want to do is direct our own paths. What we want to do is find out where we are supposed to go and what we are supposed to do. This is what concerns us. This is what overwhelms us. God says, "No, trust in Me. Lean on Me. I will do the directing."

I have fretted and worried and been consumed over direction in my life. Every time it has been unnecessary. All I needed to do was trust in the Lord and let Him bring whatever He wanted to pass. What we do is not as important as who God is.

OUR TIME WITH GOD MUST PRECEDE OUR SERVICE TO HIM

In the New Testament book of Mark chapter three, the Lord Jesus called His disciples unto Himself. He gave them a great work to do. The Bible says in Mark 3:13-14, *"And he goeth up into a mountain, and calleth unto him whom he would: and they came unto him. And he ordained twelve, that they should be with him, and that he might send them forth to preach."*

Notice that He did not first send his disciples forth to preach. First, they were to be with Him, then they could be sent forth to preach. We must get the *who* before the *what*. Some of us who are employed in the ministry have a problem. We come to church to work, not to worship. We love our work, but I am certain that sometimes we get so involved in the work that we forget the Lord of the work. Many who are not in the ministry can get in so much of a routine in service, that they lose the beautiful love for Whom they are serving.

This also happens in the home. We get so preoccupied with the things we do for the members of our family that we forget that we are doing these things because we love the people. The preciousness of our family disappears and the burden of the work appears. We must always keep *who* before *what*.

What We Have Is Not as Important as Who God Is

In Ecclesiastes 6:1 the Bible says, *"There is an evil which I have seen under the sun, and it is common among men."* It is evil and it is common. It is ordinary; it happens to everyone. What is this common evil that is among men? The Word of God says in Ecclesiastes 6:2, *"A man to whom God hath given riches, wealth, and honour, so that he wanteth nothing for his soul of all that he desireth, yet God giveth him not power to eat thereof, but a stranger eateth it: this is vanity, and it is an evil disease."*

Notice the expressions in verse two, *"God hath given,"* and *"God giveth him not."* There are things God gives us, and there are things God withholds from us. But we must realize that everything we have comes from God. Solomon said, "Here I am, the son of Bathsheba and King David. I am the king of Israel in the glory reign of the nation of Israel. I have everything at my fingertips. I am the most privileged man to ever live, but I am miserable."

Do you ever think that some people who do not know God may drive to work in the finest automobiles, sit in the finest office buildings, and go home and wish that they could just find happiness somewhere? This is the way Solomon was. He said this is common, but this is evil. He had all this opportunity and possibility, but he did not enjoy it. He was not a happy man. Solomon was learning that every ability and opportunity is a liability until it is yielded to God.

Solomon presses this point in Ecclesiastes 6:3, *"If a man beget an hundred children, and live many years, so that the days of his years be many, and his soul be not filled with good, and also that he have no burial; I say, that an untimely birth is better than he."*

This is one of the most powerful verses in the Bible. Solomon said, "Sometimes people think that if they had a family, they could get all the joy and fulfillment they could ever want just from their family." Until our children are viewed as gifts from God, they are apt to become burdens and not blessings. If you try to find all your happiness in your children and you wrap your entire life up in them, God will cause you to realize that everything about living is not in the lives of those children. It is not right for us to go through life, as God's children, without discovering that God is all-sufficient.

Solomon said, *"If a man beget an hundred children, and live many years, so that the days of his years be many, and his soul be not filled with good, and also that he have no burial..."* Solomon is speaking here of a man who never dies; he has no burial. He puts all of that on one side. On the other side, he says, *"...that an untimely birth is better than he."* What is an untimely birth? This means to be stillborn, to be born dead. The king said, "If you could have one hundred children and never die, but not know God, it would have been better to have been stillborn and never to have lived."

Do you think Solomon was right when he said that to live without God is worse than to be born dead and as a baby go into the presence of God? This is what the Bible says. To push the point further, he says in verses four and five, *"For he cometh in with vanity, and departeth in darkness, and his name shall be covered with darkness. Moreover he hath not seen the sun, nor known any thing: this hath more rest than the other."*

The only rest I find in my life is when I am trusting the Lord. There is a sweet peace and rest in faith. I have come to this conclusion: I will never find any rest, and no one else will ever find any rest until we come to the place where we say, "Lord, I am overwhelmed. All I can do is trust in You to work this out."

Until our children are viewed as gifts from God, they are apt to become burdens and not blessings.

This means that *who* God is should come before *what* we do. Perhaps you are dealing with an illness and you feel helpless. What peace can you find? The only peace you can find is in Someone, not something. Simply trust the Lord and yield your life to God.

The Bible says in verse six, *"Yea, though he live a thousand years twice told, yet hath he seen no good: do not all go to one place?"* The oldest man who ever lived was Methuselah. He lived 969 years on this earth. Solomon said, "Without Jesus Christ, living two thousand years will still not bring fulfillment. If you live two thousand years without knowing God, you have spent two thousand years not living the kind of life God wants you to live." Then he says, *"All the labour of man is for his mouth, and yet the appetite is not filled."* We all know this is true. What do we want? Just something more. Where do we want to live? Just some other place. How much money do we need? Just a little more. Without God, the appetite is never satisfied.

The Bible says in Ecclesiastes 6:8-9, *"For what hath the wise more than the fool? what hath the poor, that knoweth to walk before the living? Better is the sight of the eyes than the wandering of the desire: this is also vanity and vexation of spirit."*

This means we should learn to be content with what we have. Instead, people think, "I can never be happy here. I can never be happy with this. I can never be happy with this person. It will take something or someone else to make me happy." Many men and women have been led astray by the Devil because they were thinking such a thing. They wring their hands and say after a life of horrible regret, "I wish to God I had never made that move. I wish to God I had been faithful."

If you are not careful, you will just go round and round in life. A man in New York City said that he digs a ditch, to get the money, to get the food, to get the strength, to dig the ditch... Round and round he goes. This is all life is to most people. It may not be ditches; it may be banks, buildings, or any number of things. Without God, people are simply digging their ditch, to get their money, to get their food, to get their strength, to dig their ditch. Unless God has His proper place, life is nothing but a merry-go-round and when you get off, you are at the same place where you got on. You never will have found what Jesus Christ had for you.

> *I have found sweet peace in the Person of Jesus Christ.*

OUR GOD IS THE GOD OF THE PAST

Notice what the Bible says in the first part of verse ten, *"That which hath been is named already, and it is known that it is man."* Our God is the God of the past.

I do not want to unwind my past. God allowed me to be born to Preston Thomas Sexton and Ruby Lee Stanley Sexton. God allowed me to have a father twenty-two years older than my mother. God allowed me to go through some things in my life that are unique. God was in charge. He was still on the throne when I was born. He is the God of the past.

We can only go as far as we can get over what has already happened in our lives. We cannot change the past, but we can learn from it. We can ask God's forgiveness, and He can blot out our sins; He will wash us clean and white as snow. We can stand before God in the righteousness of Christ as if we had never been sinners. This is a wonderful promise. God is the God of the past.

I have thought so much about what a certain preacher said to me concerning my preparation for the ministry. I graduated from a secular university before I went on to seminary. He said, "That is not the kind of preparation you believe people should have. Typically you would recommend that someone preparing for the ministry should go to Bible college. Do you think you did the wrong thing?" I told him that I was not going to second-guess what God allowed me to do with my life because He is the God of the past.

Sometimes we say, "I am going to give God this, that, or the other." If we could just give God our past, some of us could be happy people again.

OUR GOD IS THE GOD OF THE PRESENT

The Bible says in Ecclesiastes 6:10-12,

> *That which hath been is named already, and it is known that it is man: neither may he contend with him that is mightier than he. Seeing there be many things that increase vanity, what is man the better? For who knoweth what is good for man in this life, all the days of his vain life which he spendeth as a*

shadow? for who can tell a man what shall be after him under the sun?

He said, *"For who knoweth what is good?"* God is the God of the present. What is it that God wants from me? He wants me right where I am, doing what I am doing, and not trying to find something else to do. He simply wants me to do my best with what I have been given right now and find my fulfillment and happiness in the Person of Jesus Christ. He is the God of the present.

Some of us are miserable because we think, "I cannot be happy now. I cannot be fulfilled now. I cannot be satisfied now. Something must change. Somebody has to go. I can never be happy at this moment." You are never happy because you are always looking for something else to make you happy. Our God is the God of the past and He is the God of the present.

OUR GOD IS THE GOD OF THE FUTURE

We see in the last part of verse twelve, *"For who can tell a man what shall be after him under the sun?"* Our God is the God of the future. My future is in God's hands.

I once heard a man give this illustration: "Can you imagine standing on top of the Grand Canyon looking down to the bottom of the canyon and watching tiny boats move through. Way out front there would be one boat. Not too far behind it there would be another. Not too far behind that one would be another. Way back in the back would be another."

Then he said, "The one in the back could not see the one in the front, but the person at the top could see the first, the last, and the middle. This is the way God looks at our lives."

We cannot understand this, but God can see the past, the present, and the future. He can see it all from His vantage point. If this is true, then why should we not trust Him and put our lives in His hands? He is the God of the future.

My past is in God's hands. He is the God of the past. He is also the God of the present and the God of the future. *Who* He is is more important than *what* I do. I have found sweet peace in the Person of Jesus Christ.

Have you ever discovered the Lord Jesus in the midst of your busy life? He is like a cool drink of water on a hot day. He is like a shady spot underneath a great oak tree when the sun has been beating down and you need a place to rest. He is like a gentle breeze when you have been scorched by the sun. If you have ever come to know the Lord and the sweet peace that only He can give, you have found that *who* He is is more important that *what* we do. Do you know Him?

Many of us need to say, "Lord, I'm going to stop making the work more important than the One for whom I am working. I am going to stop trying to find satisfaction in doing something. I am going to find my happiness and peace in knowing, loving, and worshipping the Lord Jesus Christ. I am going to do what I do because I love the Lord and I want to do it for the Lord."

Who must always come before *what*. Some of us have life out of order, and we are never going to be fulfilled until we get it right.

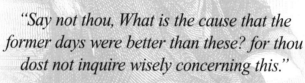

"*Say not thou, What is the cause that the former days were better than these? for thou dost not inquire wisely concerning this.*"

Ecclesiastes 7:10

Chapter Thirteen

A Better Life

 olomon tried living in the fast lane. He did everything he wanted to do, and money was no object, but this lifestyle does not last forever. Those things come to an end. This is what we see when look at this passage of Scripture.

The Bible says in Ecclesiastes 7:1-12,

> *A good name is better than precious ointment; and the day of death than the day of one's birth. It is better to go to the house of mourning, than to go to the house of feasting: for that is the end of all men; and the living will lay it to his heart. Sorrow is better than laughter: for by the sadness of the countenance the heart is made better. The heart of the wise is in the house of mourning; but the heart of the fools is in the house of mirth. It is better to*

> *hear the rebuke of the wise, than for a man to hear the song of fools. For as the crackling of thorns under a pot, so is the laughter of the fool: this also is vanity. Surely oppression maketh a wise man mad; and a gift destroyeth the heart. Better is the end of a thing than the beginning thereof: and the patient in spirit is better than the proud in spirit. Be not hasty in thy spirit to be angry: for anger resteth in the bosom of fools. Say not thou, What is the cause that the former days were better than these? for thou dost not inquire wisely concerning this. Wisdom is good with an inheritance: and by it there is profit to them that see the sun. For wisdom is a defence, and money is a defence: but the excellency of knowledge is, that wisdom giveth life to them that have it.*

Notice the phrase in the tenth verse, *"the former days were better than these."* I hear so many people talking about the "good old days," as if they would like to turn the clock back and live once again in what they refer to as the "good old days."

The Bible says in Ecclesiastes 7:10, *"Say not thou."* In other words, do not talk this way. Do not ask why the former days were better than these. There is something very dangerous about thinking this way.

There is a story in the Bible, in the fifteenth chapter of Luke, about a young man who had absolutely everything. We call it the story of the prodigal son. It is really more the story of "the loving father" than it is "the prodigal son." In this story, a young man went to his father and said he was leaving home. He did not want restraints placed on his life any longer. He asked for the portion belonging to him. Because he did not want his father telling him what to do any longer, he went his own way to do his own thing. He wasted his substance in riotous living. He came from a well-to-do home, but he came to the place where he was willing to eat what the

pigs were eating. The Bible says in Luke 15:17, *"He came to himself."* For the first time, he saw the way he had lived as God saw it. This is where everyone of us needs to come. One of the great problems in this world is that people will not take life seriously until it is nearly gone. Then they start thinking about it.

In this sermon Solomon gets serious about life. Throughout the sermon, the word *vanity* is used over thirty times. The word *vanity* means "empty." We are moving in this book now to the subject of wisdom. In the closing part of Ecclesiastes 7:12 the Bible says, *"Wisdom giveth life to them that have it."* The only place we get wisdom is from God. Jesus Christ is the wisdom of God. Wisdom is available.

> *The great lessons in life are learned in failure, not in success. Most of the great turning points in life are made during sorrow.*

Wisdom provides discernment and judgment for decision making. Decisions are more important than days. There are many people who live long lives but live them so recklessly that their lives are wasted. They make wrong decisions.

We can live a long life and make wrong decisions, and our lives will be wasted. We can live a short life and make right decisions, and our lives will accomplish much for God. It takes wisdom to make right decisions. Wisdom comes only from God. We cannot get it from Him until we come to ourselves. We must say, "Lord, I need You. I need wisdom. I need help. I need the direction that only God can give."

We think sometimes that the answer to our problems is to turn back to the "good old days." It is interesting to hear people talk about growing up during the Great Depression and talk about everything they did not have. They then say, "We had a wonderful life back then." They talk about all the heartache they went through and all the depravity they faced and then say, "Didn't we have a wonderful childhood?" Evidently, it did not seem that way at the time.

I know a young man who spent his childhood in Texas. As a young adult, his life began to fall apart. He stated often that what he needed was to get back to Texas. The truth is, what he needed was not in Texas; it was in the Lord.

Decisions are more important than days. We can live a long life and make wrong decisions, and our lives will be wasted. We can live a short life and make right decisions, and our lives will accomplish much for God.

Solomon says the temptation is to retreat to the former days. This is impossible. Sometimes we are so paranoid about the present and so fearful of the future, that the only safe place to live is in the past, but this is not God's way.

You have a rear-view mirror in your automobile, but if you try driving forward while looking in the rear-view mirror, you will end up in the hospital or dead. It does not work that way. We cannot live every day of our lives looking backward.

Memory is a beautiful thing. Jesus Christ created us with the capacity to remember. There are times He has encouraged us to remember, but He does not encourage us to live in the past. There is a difference.

As we look at the seventh chapter of Ecclesiastes, we move through a series of proverbs. Notice how often the word *better* is used. This word is mentioned in verse one, verse two, twice in verse three, verse five, twice in verse eight, and verse ten.

A Good Name Is Better

Notice verse one, *"A good name is better than precious ointment..."* *"Precious ointment"* refers to something that smells very good. Having a good name means having character, decency, and integrity. Some people are so concerned about what other people think that they are constantly pretending to be something they are not. God's emphasis in His Word is for us to be right with Him and to live lives of integrity and decency. He will take care of our names. There are many folks who are famous or have been famous who have lost their reputation and their good name. They would give anything they have to regain a good name. Guard your good name. It is better than precious ointment.

THE DAY OF DEATH IS BETTER

Verse one goes on to say, *"...and the day of death than the day of one's birth."* If you are looking at this from God's perspective and you believe that heaven is real, you know this is true. The apostle Paul said in Philippians 1:23, *"For I am in a strait betwixt two, having a desire to depart, and to be with Christ; which is far better."* Through the eyes of faith we understand that to be with Jesus Christ will be better than anything this world has to offer.

THE HOUSE OF MOURNING IS BETTER

Verse two says, *"It is better to go to the house of mourning, than to go to the house of feasting: for that is the end of all men; and the living will lay it to his heart."* In other words, it is better for us to visit a funeral than to go to a nice restaurant. There is nothing wrong with a nice restaurant, but we can learn more at the funeral. He is saying that to look at death and to experience mourning will wake us up. It will help us to get serious about life.

Many of us could mark the time and place when something tragic was used of God to change us. Most people who will not get serious about what God desires for their lives do not realize that there may be some tragedy down the road that is going to wake them up. Much wasted time will take place between now and then. The Word of God says that it is better to go to the house of mourning than to go to the house of feasting.

SORROW IS BETTER

We read in verse three, *"Sorrow is better than laughter: for by the sadness of the countenance the heart is made better."* The Bible also says in Proverbs 17:22, *"A merry heart doeth good like a medicine."* We should not be sorrowful all the time, but the Bible says here that sorrow is better than laughter. The great lessons in life are learned in failure, not in success. Most of the great turning points in life are made during sorrow. Some people think that life should just be one big party, but this is not what the Bible teaches.

The prime of life is any time in life when we are in the center of God's will.

In Ecclesiastes 2:1 Solomon said, *"I said in mine heart, Go to now, I will prove thee with mirth; therefore enjoy pleasure: and, behold, this also is vanity."* He wanted to live to enjoy, to live for pleasure. If you read in the second chapter, you will see in verse seventeen that he said, *"Therefore I hated life."*

I know men who have suffered heart attacks whose lives have been changed because of their physical calamity. They can look back and say, "I thank God for the heart attack. It made me come to my senses about something." God may use any incident in life. It may be an automobile accident; it may be the sickness of a child; it may be your own downfall; it may be some sorrow God reached down and pulled you out of, but it caused you to look back and say, "There was something in my life causing sorrow to touch my heart, and God got a hold of me."

THE REBUKE OF THE WISE IS BETTER

The Word of God says in verse five, *"It is better to hear the rebuke of the wise, than for a man to hear the song of fools."* We do not like to be rebuked, to be told where we are wrong. Until there is some rebuke, we are not going to improve; we are not going to be more like Christ. We have an old nature that rebels against rebuke. The sweetest words to our ears are the words, "You are right." The hardest words for us to hear are the words, "You are wrong."

In verse six of this same chapter, the Bible says, *"For as the crackling of thorns under a pot, so is the laughter of the fool: this also is vanity."* The crackling of thorns makes much noise, but no one benefits from it. The laughter of fools only fills the air with sound that is empty and meaningless. Satan attempts to use this to our keep minds off the serious things in life.

Our nation is as sick as it has ever been, but we are not even looking for a doctor. We are trying to patch ourselves up. We need the great Physician. Something must bring us to the place where we see that we need more than what men can do. We need what God can do. In individual lives, we must come to the place as fathers, mothers, husbands, wives, sons, and daughters where we say, "Lord, I need You!"

THE END OF A THING IS BETTER

The Word of God says in verse eight of this chapter, *"Better is the end of a thing than the beginning thereof: and the patient in spirit is better than the proud in spirit."* There is so much to learn in life. As we grow older, our energy level diminishes. What we do not have the energy to do any longer, we have urgency to help us do. We realize that we have so little of life left, and we want it to count. We begin life proud and strong, thinking we can accomplish anything. God says that *"the patient in spirit is better."*

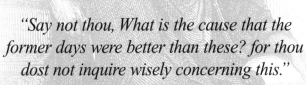

"Say not thou, What is the cause that the former days were better than these? for thou dost not inquire wisely concerning this."

Ecclesiastes 7:10

No one starts out to ruin his life, but many people have. God help us to stop reminding them of their past failures. God help all of us to leave the past.

If there are pleasant memories, then sing, "Precious memories, how they linger." We can thank God for those memories, but stop trying to dwell there. Leave the past.

LIVE IN THE PRESENT

We must live in the present. It is the only moment we have. Everything we do must be done now. If there is some restitution to be made, it must be made now. We must live in the present.

When the Twenty-third Psalm closes, the psalmist says, *"Surely goodness and mercy shall follow me all the days of my life."* The goodness and mercy of God is for the present, for this moment.

The greatest moment I have to live is now. I must make the most of what I have now. God's Word says in Matthew 6:34, *"Sufficient unto the day is the evil thereof."* There is enough to deal with each day without borrowing from yesterday or tomorrow. I must make the most of what I have now. I can throw many "nows" away by living in the past or fearing the future. I must live in the present.

You may say, "What a mess I have made." Let God use it in your life, but you do not have to make the same mess today. This is the day to trust the Lord Jesus as your Savior if you have never trusted Him. If you are not a Christian, you can become a Christian today. Ask God to forgive your sin and by faith receive Jesus Christ today. You may say, "I've carried a heavy load of unforgiveness and bitterness in my heart." I regret that you have done that, but you can get rid of the load today. The great Burden-bearer is here. The Lord Jesus says in Matthew 11:28, *"Come unto me, all ye that labour and are heavy laden, and I will give you rest."*

LOOK FORWARD TO THE FUTURE

Leave the past, live in the present, and look forward to the future. We have a great future. We do not have a fearful future. As God's children, we have a great future. The prime of life is any time in life when we are in the center of God's will.

The Bible is true. Do you believe this verse? Proverbs 4:14-15 says, *"Enter not into the path of the wicked, and go not in the way of evil men. Avoid it, pass not by it, turn from it, and pass away."*

This means to get so far away from trouble that it is not inviting. The Lord Jesus taught us to pray, *"Lead us not into temptation"* (Matthew 6:13). We should stay so far away that we are not even tempted. Proverbs 4:16-17 says, *"For they sleep not, except they have done mischief; and their sleep is taken away, unless they cause some to fall. For they eat the bread of wickedness, and drink the wine of violence."*

> The greatest moment I have to live is now. I must make the most of what I have now.

God's Word says in Hosea 8:7, *"For they have sown the wind, and they shall reap the whirlwind."* Have we not seen that if people sow to the wind, they reap a whirlwind? Have we not seen that our sins will find us out? Is there not enough evidence in our own lives of this very thing to convict us? Is there not enough evidence in the world around us to convince us that this is true?

The Bible says in Proverbs 4:18, *"But the path of the just is as the shining light, that shineth more and more unto the perfect day."* God says that the people who live for the Lord Jesus, who have trusted Christ as Savior, can count on this. Our lives will get brighter and brighter until finally we reach the perfect day. Let us learn to enjoy

the journey. As Christians, we know we will enjoy our heavenly destination, but we can also enjoy the journey.

God has given His children a beautiful future to look forward to. What about these "good old days"? We thank God we had them, but they are gone. The past is tucked away forever. We must leave the past, live in the present, and with great expectation look forward to the future. We have a wonderful Savior! Our Lord has a better life for you. It is found in Him.

Sunday School materials are available for use in conjunction with *The Conclusion of the Whole Matter*. For a complete listing of available materials from Crown Publications, please call 1-877 AT CROWN or write to: P.O. Box 159 ❖ Powell, TN ❖ 37849

Visit us on the web at
www.FaithfortheFamily.com
"*A Website for the Christian Family*"

CROWN
PUBLICATIONS
Royal Reading

OTHER SUNDAY SCHOOL MATERIALS

PILLAR AND GROUND OF THE TRUTH
SUNDAY SCHOOL SERIES

Available from CROWN PUBLICATIONS

THE LORD IS MY SHEPHERD

THE CHRISTIAN HOME

THE PARABLES OF JESUS

LORD, SEND A REVIVAL

TRUTHS EVERY CHRISTIAN NEEDS TO KNOW

ISSUES OF LIFE ANSWERED FROM THE BIBLE

EARNESTLY CONTEND FOR THE FAITH

Eight Sunday School Series Now Available!

THIRTEEN WEEKS OF BIBLE LESSONS IN EACH SERIES!

★ Full-length Book $9⁹⁵
★ Teacher's Guide $12⁹⁵
  Provided in a helpful notebook
★ Student Handbook $1⁹⁵
  For adults and teens

LET US SEND YOU A SAMPLE PACKET TODAY!
This includes a full-length book, a Teacher's Guide, and a Student Handbook for only $19.⁹⁵.

Order today on the web at FAITHFORTHEFAMILY.COM, *call* 1-877 AT CROWN, *or fax your order to us at* (865) 938-3834.